This Is How You Find Your Way

ZANNA KEITHLEY

For the soft, brave, stubborn hearts—you are worthy.

CONTENTS

INTRODUCTION

My writing journey started when I was seven years old.

I was walking through the mall with my mom, holding her hand, when we passed a Waldenbooks to the right. I turned my head and peered through the entrance and—*oh*.

That's the only way I know how to describe what that moment felt like.

Oh.

For the length of a single heartbeat, everything else disappeared. I didn't see the other mall shoppers or hear the echoes of their voices. I didn't even feel my mom's hand in mine anymore.

There was just me and that bookstore and this funny little feeling inside me.

"Mom." I turned my gaze to the mall's tiled flooring, a feeling of curiosity settling over me. "What do they call the people who write books?"

"Authors," she replied.

Authors, I repeated silently to myself. And there it was again—that odd feeling of recognition, like I'd stumbled upon something I'd been missing for a very long time. Something that held answers I didn't even know I was looking for. Something essential.

That was the moment I knew—I was going to be an author when I grew up.

From that moment on, writing became my everything. Every time I read a new book, I'd study how the author wrote dialogue and the different ways they started their stories and constructed their plots, and I practiced mimicking what they did. I filled countless notebooks with my own stories, eventually upgrading from pen and paper to my family's desktop computer. When I was twelve, I went through a brief horror genre phase, during which all my stories were set in haunted houses. Then, my focus shifted to young adult dystopian fiction throughout the rest of my teens. In college, I was able to expand my scope and learn all different types of writing—poetry and creative nonfiction and technical writing and newswriting and short fiction. I loved it all.

At 23, I graduated college with two Bachelor of Arts degrees and the dream of being a writer still very much alive in my heart.

No, not just a writer.

An *author*.

It takes a while to become an author, though. First, you have to actually write a book. Then, if you're going to follow the traditional publishing path, you need a literary agent. This means writing dozens, maybe even hundreds, of query letters, hoping just one person will see something special in you and want to represent you. Then, they have to sell your manuscript to a publisher. And then, if you're really lucky, you might be able to make enough money to call *author* your full-time career.

So after graduation, I got a job as an administrative assistant at my college town's local hospital while writing my first full-length novel manuscript in the evenings. It was set in a future world where everyone was born knowing when and how they'd one day die, and the protagonist was a sixteen-year-old girl who had less than a year to live. There was also a whole plotline about a school for kids with special abilities and another plotline about a search for a lost diamond that had magical powers. It was all very complicated, and to be honest, it wasn't very good. But for nearly two years, that book was my everything. I painstakingly edited it until I finally began to send query letters out to literary agents. For months, I'd obsessively check my email throughout the day, hoping for just one spark of hope—for one agent to say that they saw something special in my writing.

But most of the time, I'd never hear a peep. When they did respond, it was always a polite form rejection wishing me the best of luck in my search.

After a while, I finally accepted that maybe this first book manuscript wouldn't be *the one*. So, starting over again, I wrote my second manuscript. And then the third. And then the fourth.

But like the first, the next several manuscripts ultimately ended up in flash drives at the bottom of my desk drawer after a pile of rejection emails from literary agents.

Finally, after several years of pouring all my free time into my writing without seeing even a hint of promise that it was leading anywhere, I had to pause.

Doing what I had always done—immediately diving into the next project, assuming *this time, I'll finally get it right*—no longer felt like the answer.

And also—I was tired. And I was frustrated. And I wasn't having fun anymore.

Writing used to give me energy. But now, it was taking it away and leaving me feeling depleted.

All I could see from these first few unpublished manuscripts was proof of my own failure. And to be honest, I hadn't built up enough mental resilience to deal with failure very well. In my mind, these failures were a reflection of me—of my lack of worth. They showed that actually, I wasn't talented enough to make it as a writer. I wasn't anything special.

And I was certain that if other people knew about all the rejections, they'd finally see me—the real me. The me who wasn't good enough.

So I bottled up my shame and kept it buried inside me and made sure nobody found out. I didn't tell my family or friends. I told no one about the rejections and my perceived failures. In my mind, it felt safer to let them believe I wasn't actually trying that hard than for everyone in my life to know that I had tried many times and repeatedly failed.

Two decades had passed since I had walked by that Waldenbooks in the mall and *knew* I was going to be an author one day. And for the first time since that moment, something inside me began to crack.

Somewhere between all the rejections and the pressure I had put on myself to *achieve* and *succeed*, the allure of being an *author* had lost some of its magic.

I was mentally and emotionally exhausted. The constant cycle of researching literary agents, crafting unique query letters for each one, then opening up my email to find more rejections—or no response at all—was taking a toll on my mental health.

In hindsight, I can see that I was also holding onto a lot of heavy energy without having any outlets to release it. Because I refused to tell anyone about (what I perceived as) my failures, I suppressed my shame and disappointment inside myself and tried to pretend I was fine.

But when you suppress energy, it doesn't disappear. It remains stagnant within you, often manifesting into bigger issues that touch every area of your life in ways you can't always see when you're so close to it.

But I didn't know this at the time.

All I knew was that I was on the cusp of breaking and couldn't do this any longer.

So I put my projects to the side and attempted to focus on building a career outside of writing. Sometimes, a friend would ask, "Why don't you look for writing jobs?" I'd mumble a response about focusing on other things and try to change the subject quickly. But the question would repeat itself in my mind over and over again.

Why didn't I look for writing jobs?

I knew there were writing jobs I could apply for that didn't depend on manuscripts and query letters. I knew there were other potential paths, if I sought them out.

But still, if I put myself out there again, I could be rejected. And that thought alone stopped me from even trying.

It was more than just the sting of being rejected that scared me. It was what it would mean for my future. For my lifelong dream of being a writer. If I kept putting myself out there and getting turned away, eventually I'd have to accept that this dream just wasn't meant for me. I'd have to walk away from it completely.

And somewhere deep down, I wasn't ready to do that.

So the safe option was instead to not try at all.

That's the thing about dreams. When you care about something deeply, the idea of losing it is soul crushing. So it often feels easier to keep a dream tucked in your heart where it's safe and protected—where nobody can take it away from you.

Because if you actually step forward and try, but then you fail—*if it doesn't work out*—then you don't just lose the dream. You lose the hope of the dream. You can no longer say, "Well, it would've worked out if I had just tried," or, "One day, I'll go for it," always pushing that *one day* out just a little bit further.

No—you might have to admit that maybe this dream just isn't for you. You might have to let it go.

So the only way to keep it alive is to remain frozen in inaction. To never really try. To stay hidden behind *one days* and *if onlys*.

It's the same reason why you might not pursue the relationship with the person you have deep feelings for—

because as long as you never say anything, the chance of them reciprocating your feelings still exists. But if you confess your feelings and they tell you they don't feel the same, then that's it. Then you have to close the chapter on that dream.

Then you lose the hope of it all.

And losing the hope—that can be utterly devastating.

It's like standing on one side of a closed door, and on the other side are all your dreams and visions of a perfect future. You nudge the door open so you can just peek out of it, but you never quite lift your foot over the threshold.

Because if you do, someone from the other side might see you and tell you that you don't belong there.

They might push you back and slam the door in your face.

And just like that—it's over.

So for those few years, I remained firmly on my side of the door.

One day, I told myself.

One day, I'll put myself out there again.

One day, I'll try.

I continued on this path of trying to pursue some kind of career outside my childhood dream of being an author, and for a while, I could pretend I was okay with that. But in time, something shifted inside me. I realized I missed writing.

I missed the joy of it.

Because that's what it used to be—joyful.

When I was younger, I used to write as a way to explore my own imagination. Back then, I didn't expect anyone to actually *read* anything I wrote. There was no pressure to write something good that other people would deem worthy of being publishable. It was just fun. It was my creative outlet. It was pure and fulfilling. It was *mine*.

And I missed that.

I just wanted to go back to the beginning and start all over again.

So eventually, I started writing again. Not for anyone else. Just for me. I wrote poetry and short stories and even started a new novel manuscript. But this time, I had no intention of sending it to literary agents. I did it for myself. Maybe one day, I thought, if I liked it enough, I'd self-publish it, and probably only two or three people would read it, and one of those people would be my mom, and that was okay. At least then I could say I fulfilled my childhood dream of being an author, and I did it on my terms.

Meanwhile, I was still navigating what I wanted to do with my life outside of writing. After trying out a few types of jobs in different fields, I settled into a corporate job that consumed most of my mental and emotional energy. I spent my mornings getting myself worked up about whatever worst-case scenarios I imagined were going to come true that day, and I spent my evenings mentally replaying events from the day and thinking about everything that still needed to get done tomorrow.

Sometime during this period, I was talking to a friend about the stress I felt at work, and they mentioned their daily meditation practice and recommended an app I could download if I wanted to try it out. I tried it a few times but didn't really "get" it. After a few sessions of sitting cross-legged on my apartment floor, counting my breaths, I gave up.

Several months later, though, I saw the meditation app still on my phone and decided to give it another try. This time, I tried different types of meditation. When I discovered visualization meditation, something finally clicked. I found myself actually looking forward to my daily meditation sessions. I listened to guided visualization meditations that led me down different types of journeys. Sometimes, they'd take me back to my past—back to moments when I felt scared, embarrassed, hurt, and alone. And in those moments, my current self would give my inner child the nurturing and compassion she so badly wanted but hadn't known how to ask for back then.

Most often, though, I'd visualize my future.

What did I want? Who did I want to be? Where did I want to go? What did my dream *tomorrow* look like?

What I discovered was that no matter what version of the future I visualized, there was always one common theme that appeared throughout all my visions: writing.

As scared as I was of getting that one final rejection that would act as proof that I wasn't meant to be an author, there was still a tiny spark of belief within me.

I still believed I could do this.

I still believed this dream was meant for me.

In one of my visualizations, I returned to that moment in the mall with my mom when I was seven years old. Except I wasn't seven years old anymore. I was the current me, standing next to the seven-year-old me. I faced the bookstore and took my younger self's hand and squeezed it softly. And I made her a promise.

I promised my younger self that I wouldn't give up on our dream.

I still didn't know how exactly I was going to do it. Every time I thought about returning to the cycle of writing fiction manuscripts and querying literary agents, something inside me would shut down. I was playing around with writing fiction for fun, but the idea of becoming a novelist just wasn't clicking anymore. The problem was, when I tried to think of other possibilities for my writing career, I had a hard time finding a path that felt right to me.

So I kept meditating.

I returned to meditation over and over again, sometimes sitting in silence, and other times letting another's voice guide me on a deeply personal inner journey. I loved the guided visualization meditations and wanted to learn more about terms I kept hearing like *manifestation* and *Law of Attraction*. So in my free time, I read everything I could find about manifesting methods and the science behind manifestation and how energy worked. I created daily practices rooted in gratitude and positive affirmations. I experimented with different journaling methods and became acutely aware of my own vibration.

Nothing changed overnight, but in hindsight, I can look back and see the shift that gradually unfolded over the next few months. After years of tunnel vision and not seeing any possibilities for building a writing career outside of writing novels, I started to get ideas.

Finally, a potential path was beginning to open up for me.

I already had the domain *zannakeithley.com* for building my writer portfolio. Besides some basic contact information, it had nothing on it. I had never spent any time working on the website before, but now, I found myself thinking about it constantly.

What if I actually added content to the site, I thought. Like a blog.

A blog that could maybe even help people like me.

People who were a little lost and just trying to find something. A spark of hope. An inspired idea. Something *more*.

I could write about manifestation and share all the affirmations I used and even add more content about the other practices that had helped me along the way, like meditation and journaling and chakra healing.

So I started to research everything I could find on blogging: what I needed to do, how to choose topics to write about, how to get people to actually read my blog posts.

Pretty quickly, I realized that if I was serious about wanting to grow my blog, I'd need some kind of social media to go with it.

And *this*—this almost scared me more than getting another rejection.

Honestly, this almost made me quit before I had even started.

My social media experience was close to nonexistent. I've always been an intensely private person. This comes from a deep need to remain safe and guarded. Not being active on social media was how I protected myself. As a sensitive person who feels a lot of big feelings, I wasn't sure I could handle the not-so-great parts of building a social media platform.

Mostly, though, it came down to one thing.

I was absolutely terrified of being seen.

So I meditated on it. I journaled about it daily. I took daily walks around my neighborhood, replaying the same thoughts and questions in my head.

Could I really put myself out there on social media? Could I share my thoughts and feelings and ideas publicly? How would I feel if someone left me a negative comment? Would I be able to handle it? Was I actually ready to step out of this safe, protective shell I'd wrapped myself in?

Could I allow myself to be seen?

These questions circled through my mind repeatedly.

And I kept coming back to the same answer.

As scary as it was, I had to give it a chance.

I had to try.

I thought that was going to be the hardest decision I had to make—choosing to set up social media accounts for my blog and putting myself out there in a way I never had before. But soon, another seed was planted in my consciousness and began to grow roots. An idea that wasn't even a tiny bit reasonable.

To go all in on my writing, I needed to quit my full-time job.

Now, if you ask me to give you advice on what to do if you're in a similar situation—well, first, I'll always tell you to follow what feels right for you, regardless of anything I say.

But if I really had to give an answer, I'd tell you that quitting your job when you're reliant on that income to pay your bills and you have no idea how you're going to make money probably isn't the best idea.

And my rational, logical mind knew that. Even if I started blogging on my website and tiptoed into the world of social media, I'd still have to figure out a way to produce some kind of income. I had no platform, no portfolio, no connections. The option of quitting my job shouldn't have even been on the table.

This inner voice that existed beyond my rational mind, though—it didn't care. It just kept getting louder and more persistent. And this feeling deep inside that *I had to do this* wouldn't go away. And the more I tried to overpower it with logic and reason, the stronger it became.

So again, I meditated on it. Over and over again, day after day.

The thing about meditation is that for a while, it feels like nothing is happening. I don't think I've ever ended a meditation session just suddenly *knowing* all the answers to all my questions. It's not like a fast-food restaurant where I can put in an order for life guidance and get served instantly with a robust serving of clarity.

No—it's always been more like a gradual dawning. Most of the time, I don't even realize it's happening. I just keep returning to the practice each day, and in time, the noise of the outside world gets a little quieter. New ideas come. Previously unseen paths make themselves known. And I can feel that thing deep within. A kind of internal guidance system that says—*go this way*.

I still didn't have any answers about how I was going to make money and support myself. But I kept coming back to the same word:

Trust.

So finally, after a few months of spinning in circles in my mind, I did it. I gave my notice to my boss.

Two weeks later, I published my first blog post and posted on Instagram for the very first time. I was so wound up after pressing the *Publish* button that I immediately put on my running shoes and ran six miles that went by in such a blur, when I looked down at my watch and saw how far I had run, I remember feeling shocked because I felt like I'd only been running for a few minutes.

Initially, my plan was to focus mainly on my blog and use Instagram to support my website. I never planned on posting my original prose as the main image on my Instagram posts. Instead, I searched for really great quotes from other writers and created designs that highlighted *their* words, crediting them, and posted those as the main images on my feed. Then, in the caption, I'd talk about what the quote meant to me or give a personal anecdote that was related to the meaning of the quote.[1]

In time, I discovered that people seemed to be resonating with the captions I wrote for the quotes that I shared on my feed. Writing captions was actually the part of the process I enjoyed the most. It felt like a low-pressure way to share my words without worrying about being perfect. Slowly, I learned how to let down my guard and become more vulnerable. And the more vulnerable I was, the more people seemed to connect with what I was writing. And eventually, I realized that I didn't need to offer a perfectly curated version of myself. I didn't always need things to be pretty. I just needed to be honest. And the more honest I was, the more my writing seemed to connect.

Writing these captions led me to playing around with

---

[1] The rest of this introduction is going to focus more on my Instagram journey than my blogging and freelance writing path, so to give you a brief rundown of what happened next—I spent the next several months writing and publishing posts on my blog to build a writing portfolio. Then, I started applying for freelance writing positions, ultimately landing a contract ghostwriting position where I was able to write blog articles, digital workbooks, and online courses for a spirituality and self-care website. I then began working full-time for a B2B content company while continuing to focus on my own writing projects on the side. Ultimately, that gentle nudge to trust hadn't steered me wrong.

writing short prose pieces in my spare time. I had a morning journaling practice, and each morning, I began asking, *what's the truest thing I know right now?*

The answer would change each day.

Sometimes, the truest thing I knew was that something in my heart was telling me it was time to make a big change, but I felt scared and was resisting change because I wasn't sure I was ready.

Sometimes, the truest thing I knew was that I felt sad and a little lost and homesick for a home I wasn't sure I'd ever known.

Sometimes, it was simply that I was grateful. Sometimes, this feeling of gratitude permeated so deeply that it felt like it was the only thing that existed.

It wasn't always so deep, though. Some days, I'd spend the entire journaling session writing about how tired I felt or rambling about my writer's block. It didn't matter if what I wrote in my journal entries was profound or even good. It just had to be true.

I began taking these journal entries and creating short prose pieces out of them. Initially, I didn't plan on sharing these pieces with anyone. This was just a way for me to practice my writing and explore how to become more vulnerable through my words.

But in time, that inner feeling returned. The gentle nudge. That thing that said—*go this way.*

I resisted at first. Putting my words at the forefront of my Instagram posts had never been my intention. My voice was hidden in the captions. It was never meant to take center stage.

So once again, I meditated on it.

This time, I kept coming back to a single three-letter word:

Try.

Just try.

So finally, I climbed out from the caption and started posting my own prose as the main image on my Instagram posts.

Was all of it good? Absolutely not.

In the beginning, I was hard on myself when I'd reread a piece I had published and saw places where the writing could've been improved. But in time, I realized—that was kind of the point.

The fact that I could look back at work I'd done and spot weaknesses in my own writing meant I was growing as a writer. This was a good thing. It meant I was on the right path.

At the time, my audience was tiny, which meant I had the time and freedom to discover my voice and connect deeper with myself and my writing on a very small platform. The biggest lesson I learned was that I was never going to write something that could please everyone. And if I tried to write something for everyone, ultimately, it'd be for no one.

So instead, I focused on just one person. If I could write something meaningful for just one person, if just one person was listening, if something I wrote sparked something that made a difference in the heart of just one person—then that was enough.

But eighteen months after my very first Instagram post, something began to shift.

Somehow, more people were finding my words.

I'm not a numbers and data person, and I've always avoided looking at social media analytics because they stress me out. But it was impossible to not notice the drastic increase that seemed to be happening out of nowhere. More people reaching out. More people stumbling across my writing. Just more people, everywhere.

And then, on an unassuming Friday morning, I posted a short piece with a golden yellow background that started with three simple words: *Actually, you can.*

I had just finished editing the post right before I published it. When I hit the *Publish* button, I didn't think anything of it. I put my phone down and continued with my to-do list for the day. Later, when I opened the Instagram app again, I noticed the like count was way higher than usual. And throughout the day, every time I'd go back, the likes had increased by hundreds. And hundreds more. Then, thousands.

Over the next several days, that post received tens of thousands of likes, and my follower count went from less than 4,000 to over 14,000.

It was my first experience having a post go viral, and I almost deactivated my entire account the very next week.

What should've been an exciting moment sent me into a month-long anxiety spiral. In hindsight, I can pinpoint it all back to that one fundamental fear that I'd never fully overcome: being seen.

This fear was the root of all my other fears. The fear of not being good enough. The fear that I wasn't worth people's time. The fear that I wasn't worthy of this newfound attention.

The fear that once people began to really see me, they'd all turn away.

I woke up each morning with pressure in my chest that only went away when I was sleeping. I thought about deactivating my account about a thousand times.

So again, I returned to meditation.

And I'd meditate daily, often multiple times a day. And I tried to find some kind of guidance, some kind of direction—something to make me feel like this sudden success wasn't going to swallow me whole.

And finally, after about a month of feeling frozen in my own anxiety and fear, three words began to echo softly in my mind:

I'll be okay.

That was it. I know it doesn't sound like much. Three tiny words. A few letters and syllables.

But those words were the only thing that somehow pierced through all the anxiety and gave me some kind of

15

relief. My throat finally opened up again. The weight on my chest lifted.

I could breathe.

In those three words, I realized there was an infinite number of possibilities for my future, and while some of it was in my control, most of it wasn't. Maybe I'd never write anything good again. Maybe my biggest fear would come true—maybe people would see, I mean *really see* me, in that way so many of us desperately want to be seen but are also completely and utterly terrified of. And maybe when they did, they'd decide they didn't like what they saw. Maybe they'd leave. Maybe I'd lose it all.

And I realized that if that happened—I'd be okay.

Those external circumstances had no power over me unless I gave them power.

And if it all went away tomorrow, that's because it wasn't meant for me. And that was okay. I trusted the universe. I trusted my path. Even if this specific dream didn't work out, I'd find another one. I'd keep leaning into my heart's wisdom. I'd believe in something bigger than myself, bigger than all of this.

Since that moment, those three words have been my anchor, not just with my writing career but with all aspects of my life.

When I want to control a situation and realize I can't control it and that I have to trust, I take a deep breath and remind myself—I'll be okay.

And when I'm about to do something that terrifies me and I'm tempted to turn back and return to my comfort zone, I say it again—I'll be okay.

And when things are actually going well and I start to worry about it all disappearing, I have to tell myself that if it does disappear, it's because the universe has a different plan for me.

And again—I'll be okay.

The path from that moment to publishing this book has been anything but linear. The thing I've learned about following your dreams and trusting the whispers of your inner guidance system is that it often requires you to break your own heart, over and over again. To make space for what's for you, you have to be willing to let go of what isn't. Connections. Attachments. People and things and experiences that maybe were meant to be for a brief moment in time but weren't meant to be forever.

Still, even in the deepest trenches of grief, something deep inside of me has always known—I'll be okay.

And if you take only one thing with you from this entire book, I hope it's that.

I hope you know you'll be okay.

There's going to be a lot to navigate as you walk this heart-led path. And you're not always going to be able to see what's coming. Your rational mind might think it knows best, but there are things happening beyond your scope of vision that are working in the background. Things the rational mind can't see. And it's so easy to say *just trust* and so incredibly hard to actually do it. Especially when everything feels like it's going wrong. When it feels like you're pouring your whole heart into something and nothing is working out. When you're tired, frustrated, sad, heartbroken, and angry at the universe for seemingly always working against you.

I promise—you're going to be okay.

It won't always feel like it. But if you can begin to build that into your foundation and keep coming back to it and keep coming back to it and keep coming back to it, it's going to ground you. And in those three words—*I'll be okay*—you cultivate trust. Trust in yourself. Trust in your heart. Trust in the universe.

If I could go back to the beginning and tell myself anything, that's what I would say.

You'll be okay.

I don't think there's anything else I could've said that would've had a more meaningful impact than those words. It's a quiet confidence. A soft courage. Just knowing that whatever fears you're walking towards, whatever uncertainties exist on the unknown trail ahead, you're going to make it. You'll be okay.

This path is going to take you to places you never once imagined. Just by following your heart and exploring your potential and giving yourself a chance, you'll experience a fullness of life that you didn't know existed. And one day, you're going to know that incredible feeling of achieving a goal you weren't sure you'd reach. Of a dream actually coming true. Of the universe opening up for you and dazzling you with its magic.

But that won't be the end.

The path will continue. It'll expand, and there will be new goals. New dreams. New possibilities.

And that's why it's so important to remember—you can't wait.

You can't wait until you reach the destination to allow yourself to feel everything you want to feel in life.

All the joy. All the gratitude. All the love.

Because there will always be a new destination to replace the old one. Your life journey is continuous and ever evolving. And all the tiny miracles and hidden wonders—they're not waiting there at the end of it all. They're here, in the journey.

And you are worthy of experiencing it all. Not just in some distant future you keep imagining for yourself but here. Right here. This heartbeat is just as worthy of knowing true bliss as the next. This breath is just as worthy of being loved as the one that follows.

You are worthy.

You're worthy of living the most honest, fulfilling, and beautiful life you can imagine for yourself.

You're worthy of living a life that aligns with your soul's deepest truth.

You're worthy of this dream that's been placed in your heart.

You. You're worth everything.

* * *

This book is for anyone who wants to pour their whole heart into the act of living.

Our time here isn't very long. Months turn into years which turn into decades that pass by so incredibly fast.

In the beginning, we spend a lot of time learning how to be good, respectable humans. How to act. How to communicate. How to listen and follow rules and not get into trouble. We learn the "right" way to do things—the right way to live and think and be. We follow these rules that we're told are *right*, that sound *right*, mostly because people who are older than us are telling us they are *right*.

And as we get a little older, we learn a new set of rules—the rules of self-preservation.

Don't text back too quickly. Hold your cards close. Play it cool. Vulnerability is a weakness. Don't let anyone discover your soft heart. Place your feelings in a box and stash it somewhere deep inside yourself so no one will ever know how much and how deeply you feel. Dreams are nice, but practicality is better. Failure is bad. Rejection is worse. If you don't put yourself out there, you'll never have to experience the pain of either one.

These rules become the stories we tell ourselves as we navigate our paths and try to do the best we can with what we have. And for a while, these stories seem good. They seem right.

Until one day.

One day, when you realize that the stories you've been clinging onto no longer support you. That they're holding you back. Keeping you stuck.

That they're preventing you from putting yourself out there and doing the things that excite you—that they're stopping you from walking toward the life that's calling to you.

And when you really start to dig deeper into these stories, you realize that at the root of them all, is fear. Fear of rejection. Fear of failure. Fear of being hurt. Fear of messing up. Fear of other people's opinions.

And maybe you don't want to live in fear anymore.

Maybe—maybe you just want to live.

This book is for the person who's ready to let go of the worn-out stories of the past and step into something new. Something kind of scary but also exciting. For the person who doesn't want to spend their entire life hiding in the shadows. For the person who wants to see what they can do with the decades they have in front of them.

For the person who just wants to live.

Maybe you're already there. And if you are, this book is for you, too. For the person who has already made quiet steps and big leaps. For the person who continues to show up for themselves, day after day.

Maybe you're starting to witness some of the rewards of your perseverance. Or maybe it still feels like you're taking more steps backward than forward.

But still—there's a pull in your heart and an inner voice that keeps whispering, *keep going.* So you do, even when you're uncertain where it's all leading—if it's even leading anywhere at all.

This book is for you.

For anyone who doesn't want to reach the end of their life and think, *"I wish I would've..."*

I wish I would've written the book. I wish I would've performed in public. I wish I would've asked that person out. I wish I would've gone back to school. I wish I would've put myself out there. I wish I would've explored my passions. I wish I would've gotten over my pride and just tried.

For anyone who is currently walking down this heart-led path but still pauses several times a day, questioning whether they can really do this. For anyone who is currently living in the space between hope and fear. For anyone who has ever experienced friction between their head and their heart. I hope you find what you need in these pages.

And for anyone who isn't sure of anything except for *this feeling*.

This feeling that tells you that you have to find out what's on the other side of this path. You have to know. You have to see where it leads.

This book is for you.

Is it going to be easy? No. But you probably already know that. Because nobody who takes the heart-led path does it because they think it's going to be easy.

They do it because there is no other choice. Others may not always understand. They may call it reckless, foolish, illusory, a fairy tale.

But for you, it's the most real thing that exists.

This book is for the dreamers and the doers. For the people who have big dreams and take actionable steps to make their visions come true. For the people who know that what they have to offer matters. That it's important. That by trusting their heart's guidance, they have something meaningful to share with the world.

For you—the one who is awakening to the power of your own magic.

This is how you find your way.

PART 1: THIS IS FOR REMEMBERING YOUR MAGIC

You don't always see your own magic because it's disguised in the ordinary things you do every day. It's the way you see the world. How you make others feel when they're in your presence—like they're *seen*. Like they matter. Like they're accepted, just as they are. It's the revolution inside you that says *maybe the way things have always been* isn't the way they *have to be*. How you're willing to make a new path. To go in a different direction. To follow the call of your wild heart. It's your inner spark that radiates outward and lights up a room. It's your stubbornness and how you'll never give up on what's most important to you: people, beliefs, goals, dreams. You're not fearless, but you're willing to face your fears for the things that matter. And when the world tells you to be mean, you lean deeper into kindness. When the world tells you not to love, you love harder. Cynicism would be easy, but you've never taken the easy road. On those heavy nights when the world is immersed in darkness, you'll still be the last spark of hope. All this time, you've been searching for magic in the world outside of you, but can't you see it yet? You *are* the magic.

And all I can ask is when I tell you that you are a gift, that you don't roll your eyes and brush it off like you're nothing special. That you listen. Just this once. Just listen. I know how easy it is to hear those words and think, *No, not me. Those words aren't meant for me.* But when I say *you are a gift*, I mean that your smile has the power to lift a person's entire day. That your willingness to just be there and listen can pull someone from the brink of darkness and remind them that there is *light* and *good* and *beauty* in this world. That I know you don't let everyone in, but for the ones you do— it is an *honor*. And when I say *you are a gift*, I mean there's something inside you that this world needs: words and art, advocacy and mentorship, compassion and love. That what you create through your fingers and voice and body has the power to shatter through the numbness and make someone *feel*. When I say *you are a gift*, I mean there are sparks of your magic planted throughout this world from words you've said, kindness you've offered, art you've created. That you matter in ways you may never fully comprehend. You walk through life making everything around you a little more beautiful. And you may not always see it, but who you are—your mind, your heart, the energy you carry into every new experience—that's your gift.

Things you need to hear: first, you're enough. You. Exactly as you are. Don't hide your true self to be accepted. Don't alter your energy to be loved. That's not real acceptance. That's not real love. And my goodness, you are so worthy of the real thing. You're worthy of being seen. Being known. And being valued for everything that makes you *you*—even those parts you've tried to suppress and hide. Please know—nothing about you needs to be hidden. Nothing about you is a mistake. Yes, over time, you're going to change and transform. You'll shed layers of your past self as you continue on this lifelong journey of self-discovery and growth. But the core of who you really are? Your divine essence? Every strange, quirky, beautiful thing that makes you uniquely you? That's yours for keeps. And it's worth loving. Honoring. Protecting. And anyone who is truly meant to walk beside you on this path is going to love and protect it, too. And can't you see? That's worth waiting for. That's worth staying true to yourself for. *That*—it's worth everything.

For those days when you wish you could be a little less *you* and more like somebody else, I hope you can take a deep breath and remember—your authentic self is worthy of being seen. Of being known. Of being felt. Of being heard. Of being here, on this earth. Exactly as you are. You're not simply taking up space. You're adding to it. Enhancing it with your energy. *Making it greater.* And your authentic self is worthy of knowing deep and real love. Your authentic self is worthy of experiencing pure, unfiltered connection. Your authentic self is worthy of encountering every treasure this world has to offer. Of knowing what it feels like when a dream comes true. Of living a vast, meaningful, fulfilling life. And that starts with you. It starts with *choosing your authenticity* over *everything else.* It starts with saying no to anything that doesn't settle just right in your bones. It starts with staying true to you, regardless of what others may think. This world doesn't need less of you. It needs more. More of your energy. More of your spirit. More of your everything.

Actually, your world does revolve around you—it must. In your story, you're the earth *and* the sun. This means you must tend to your own soil before you can help another with theirs. You must water your own flowers first. You must be the moon and the stars, shining light into your darkness, and you must be the stillness that calms your own storms. So give yourself permission to put yourself first without asking for forgiveness. Allow yourself to contract before you expand. Step inside yourself and stay there for a while. Offer this as your gift to the world: you, fully bloomed, with an inner world so radiant, it spills outside of yourself and spreads light to everything it touches.

And maybe it's time to let the honey-soaked syllables of your favorite love poem wrap around your heart and teach you how to feel again. Maybe it's time to give yourself the love you've been waiting for *out there*. Maybe it's time to whisper sweet nothings into your own ear. To make your own self-promises. To write an unbreakable oath of deep, unconditional self-love. Maybe it's time to let the gentle melodies of your favorite love song spill into your bloodstream and feed every neglected part of you. Maybe it's time to stop picking at the wounds on your skin and instead pick at the wounds that have been living inside you all these years. Maybe it's time to feel what you need to feel so you can finally release it. Maybe it's time to go deeper. To love yourself harder. To break down so you can break open. To find every broken fragment inside of you and gently carry it to the surface. To let your whole self be seen. Heard. Known. Understood. Accepted. Loved.

And I know that after all this time, you're still trying to regain your balance. Trying to settle into a new chapter that has looked and felt different than all the ones before. And you keep trying to move forward by trying to go back. Back to when things were simpler. Easier. When you didn't have to try so hard to be *you*. When you could just *be*. Because that's what this is all about, isn't it? You're still trying to be the *you* from the past. The *you* that hadn't walked through the fire. The *you* that felt effortless. The better, more preferable *you*. And I know that you closed your petals and shrank into yourself, retreating to the safest place you could find. And you keep waiting for the *old you* to return so you can open up again. But I hope you know—you have permission to release that weight. To let go of any expectations that you're supposed to be exactly as you were back then. The *old you* wasn't better. The *old you* wasn't wiser. The *old you* didn't have anything you don't have now. You hold so much strength and wisdom inside yourself that you didn't know back then. And I hope you can let your petals unfold as you meet this next version of yourself. Because what's blooming is more exquisite and unique than you can possibly imagine. And who you are today—*who you are always*—is worth your unshakeable love.

You are worthy of the same love you so willingly give to others. You are worthy of the same forgiveness you so easily bestow upon others. You are worthy of the same compassion you so effortlessly hold for others. And the time and energy you dedicate to everyone else? You're worthy of saving some of it for yourself, too. Whenever you find yourself drowning beneath self-criticism, ask yourself, *would I speak to someone I love this way?* It's so easy for you to say that your friends deserve love. That your family deserves happiness. That people you've never even met deserve to live beautiful lives. You freely grant these gifts upon everyone else without a second thought. So why can't you extend this same kindness to yourself? Nobody is criticizing you the way *you* criticize you. This entire universe is waiting for you to see your own potential. This world wants to see you shine.

You are not hard to love. You are not a burden. You are not trouble. You are not a lost cause. You are not a sum of the labels that have been given to you. You are not hopeless. You are not second best. You are not a problem. Nothing about you is wrong. Nothing about you is lesser. *Nothing about you is a mistake.* And if they made you feel that way, I promise—it wasn't you. It was never you. Because you were never hard to love. They just had a hard time loving themselves. You were never unworthy. They just had a hard time believing in their own worthiness. You were never mediocre. They just couldn't support your dreams because that meant acknowledging that they'd forgotten their own. They didn't want to recognize your magic because they were afraid they'd lost theirs. It was easier to try to suppress your light than to admit they were living in the dark. So please—don't let them stop you. Don't let them take away your spark. Take a deep breath and remember who you are: you are easy to love, filled with potential, and *a gift* to this world.

I think it's time. After all these years of holding the heavy weight of your own expectations on your shoulders. You've been fighting never-ending battles in your mind for so long. Always finding *one more thing*. One more thing about yourself to focus on. One more thing to improve. One more thing to fix. And you think—*Maybe then I'll be happy. Maybe then I'll be free. Maybe then, finally, I'll be able to breathe.* But I promise—what you're seeking isn't down that path. Love doesn't exist in a state where it requires you to become something better in order to receive it. And what you're seeking isn't going to be found in the next, leveled-up version of you. It's here. Right here. Piercing through you right now. The love you need is the love you have. The acceptance you're looking for is the acceptance you can give. The approval you're seeking is your own. And I think, finally, after all these years—it's time. You don't need to keep chasing these ever-elusive states of perfection. You don't need to chase a thing. Because what you're searching for—you already have it. It's in your mind and body and the untamed heart beating inside your chest. It's in you.

Do you know how desperately the world wants to see you? To know you. To experience you. *You*. Just as you are. You, in all of your light. You—an original. You shake your head. You tell yourself there's no way that out of the billions of people on this planet, *you* could be something special. You think it's inconceivable that you could hold something meaningful inside yourself that nobody else can offer—that nobody has ever possessed before and nobody will ever possess again. But I promise—you were created exactly as you are because everything you are is everything this world needs. You're not an imposter. You're not second best. You're it. Unrivaled. Unparalleled. Second to none. And that *thing* you possess inside yourself? The voice that's uniquely. Your natural talents. The knowledge you've gained from experiences that only *you* have lived. All of these aspects of yourself that make you *uniquely you* are everything this world is seeking. Can you feel it when you close your eyes? The energy of the universe flowing through you. You're the magic. You're the spark. You're the gift.

Remove the word *just* from your vocabulary when you're describing yourself. You are not *just* an artist. Not *just* a creator. You are not *just* a coach or a teacher. Not *just* an entrepreneur. You are not *just* a dreamer. Not *just* someone who is a little lost and still trying to figure this whole living thing out. Can't you see? You are not *just* anything—you are *everything*. Those little nudges you feel pointing you in a certain direction? The pull inside your heart? The call you hear deep within your soul? That indescribable feeling of *rightness* guiding you forward? That's the entire universe flowing through you. You are powerful beyond measure. Your light is the same light that illuminates the night sky. Your breath is the same breath that sweeps over the ocean. Nothing about you can be described with the word *just*. You are expansive. You are limitless. You are infinite. You are *more*.

Do you know how many times you asked if you were *worthy* of the thing you really wanted, when all along, you were actually *overqualified* for the position? Do you know how many times the person on the other side of the table was *thanking the universe* that you showed up? Do you know how many prayers you've answered? Do you realize what a gift you are? Can you see yourself the way others see you? Can you comprehend just how effortlessly your magic flows? Do you know how desperately this world needs you? Do you have any idea just how brilliantly you shine? Can you recognize how *nobody else* in the world has what you have? Can you see how invaluable you truly are? Please don't spend an entire lifetime questioning whether you're worthy of this world's time and attention. Can't you see it yet? Can't you feel it? How *who you are* and *what you have to offer* is exactly what this world is searching for.

Do you know that you light up every room you walk in? Do you know how good you make people feel? Do you know that your smile is like pure sunlight? That your laugh vibrates straight into a person's bones and becomes the best part of their day? Do you have any idea how radiant you are? How you shine? How you glow? Do you know how much someone out there looks forward to the moment when they get to see you—when they get to experience just *a little bit* of your light? You love fiercely. You give openly. You do *so much* for *so many* without ever asking for anything in return. And *I know*. I know you hide your pain so effortlessly. That you pour your energy into making other people feel good so they'll never have to feel the way you've felt. So they'll never feel so alone. And I hope you know—you are a gift. An unmatched, irreplaceable gift. You are so incredibly important. And the parts of you that you don't think are worthy of receiving love? Your shadows. Your darkness. Your pain. I promise you—they are. Every part of you is equally worthy: your darkness and your light. All of you has value. All of you is enough. All of you is worthy of being loved.

I hope you know that your heart is enough. You're smart enough and funny enough and interesting enough. Your smile is enough. Your light is enough. And the parts of you that you struggle with and try to hide—they're enough, too. And if you just want to sit for hours and not say a single word, your presence is enough. You don't have to talk to fill the noise. You don't have to say anything at all. Just stay true to yourself. Offer who you are, not who you think the world wants you to be. Because I promise—your heart is enough. You're enough. You have nothing to prove.

You are someone's favorite person. You're the best part of their day. You're the thing that keeps them going. You're their deep, soulful sigh of relief. You're the breath of fresh air they take after a long day of walking through crowded rooms and confined spaces. You're the sunbeam that pierces through gray skies. You're a safe place to land. The one visible star on a cloudy night. The way home. And I know there are days when you feel lost and uncertain of your place in this world. You may feel like nothing you do or say makes a difference. But I hope you know that *you are a gift* to every single person who has the honor of experiencing *just a fraction* of your light. Your presence is both the most grounding and uplifting thing in this world. And you are so incredibly vital and necessary and important. You're it. You're the one. You're everything.

If I could tell you one thing, I would tell you that you are worthy. You're worthy of living a life that feeds your spirit and nourishes your soul. You're worthy of knowing love and acceptance every single day, in every single way. And you're worthy of these deep-rooted dreams and visions inside yourself that you just can't shake. Or maybe—maybe I'd tell you that the right people will fall hopelessly in love with your brand of *weird* and *unique*. That you don't need to alter the core of who you are to be loved because the core of who you are is so hauntingly special. And the right people will see that. They'll feel it. You don't have to convince them of anything. Or maybe I'd tell you to just go for it. The job. The relationship. Find the thing that feels like *love* and *freedom* and *truth* and go that way. Or maybe I'd just tell you that you are a gift. Maybe I'd beg you not to settle. Or maybe—maybe I wouldn't say anything at all. Maybe your heart already knows what you need to hear. And maybe all I can do is look you in the eyes and show you—*I see you*. And I'm so glad you're here. I've been so desperate to know you. And I think you're the best thing this universe has ever made.

The truth is, you were never meant to fit in. I know for so many years, those were the worst possible words you could've heard. You spent your whole life feeling like you never really belonged. Always playing catch up. Forever trying to mold yourself into what you thought everyone else wanted. Into what you thought was *right* and *acceptable*. Into what you thought would earn you love. But my goodness, can't you see? You don't have to earn a thing. *You are already right and acceptable.* You are this beautiful, rare, irreplaceable gift. You may have forgotten your magic somewhere along the way, but you never lost it. It shines through your eyes and flows through your fingertips and leaves its mark on every person who has the honor of knowing you. And I hope you can walk into every room knowing *you belong here.* I hope when you look at the sunsets and wildflowers and ocean waves, you remember that the beauty you see *out there* is a reflection of the beauty that exists within you. I hope you spend the rest of your life adoring every quirky and unique and different thing that makes your presence so magnetic. You were never meant to fit in, and *thank goodness.* Thank goodness you're here. Thank goodness you exist.

You are not simply a sum of your achievements. You're not a number or a label. You're not a math problem to be solved or a word in a dictionary that comes with a neat, tidy, unchanging definition. And my goodness—you are not a house whose value is appraised through comparisons and curb appeal. Your worth can't be devalued due to the parts of you that you deem broken. You're not for sale. You don't need to be fixed. You are a living, breathing, conscious human being who has no value because you are *invaluable*. Your worth can't be assessed because it's not a contract that comes with fine print or stipulations. It's permanent. Ingrained into your very being. Don't you see? You affirm that *you're enough* like it's your lifeline, but *enough* is the smallest thing about you. Of course you're enough, but also—you're *so much more*. And it's unfathomable to think that you—an immeasurable soul who has the universe's eternal breath flowing through your lungs and its inextinguishable light illuminating each and every cell inside your body—could ever be anything less than endlessly and undeniably worthy of every single thing you've ever dreamed about. And that's just the beginning. Do you know that yet? *That's just the beginning.*

They say that to have it, you must become it. To have love, you must become love. To have success, you must become success. To have what you desire most, you must become the embodiment of that thing. But that's not really what it's all about. It's about realizing *you already are it*. You are the love. You are the success. You are the peace, the abundance, the spark of hope you've been waiting for. You are the magic. You are the light. The seeds of everything you're searching for have already been planted inside you. It's not about *becoming* anything. It's about letting go of everything that blocks you from the truth. It's about realizing that *the thing* you seek is already an inextricable part of your being. You don't have to search. You don't have to beg. You don't have to wait. Everything you've been looking for—it's within you.

Who are you really? In your heart. At your core. Visualize a life of pure freedom. Freedom from limits and constraints. From worry and fear. From *the thing* that makes you feel stuck and unable to move forward. Imagine yourself in the place where you feel most alive: walking through the wildflowers, standing on top of a mountain, lost in the ocean waves. See yourself as you really are. The truest, most authentic you. The unbroken you. The uncaged you. The abundant you. Now, your brain might start to protest. It may say, *"But I can't be that person because . . ."* And that's okay. Show yourself grace. But what if just for today, you consciously turned that story around? What if today, instead of listing all the reasons why you can't be that person, you sought out the reasons why you can? What if instead of looking for limits, you searched for possibilities? What if just for today, you remained open? Open to new opportunities. To unimagined possibilities. To once-in-a-lifetime chances and beautiful beginnings. And what if today, you told yourself a different story? A story of promise. Of hope. A story that begins, *Actually, I can . . .*

Don't settle. Please. Not anymore. Maybe once upon a time, you convinced yourself that it isn't so bad to settle. That maybe you could learn to be okay with a life that doesn't nourish your soul—a life that doesn't pour back into you all that you pour into it. And you talked yourself into believing that maybe it was *too much* to think that you should be hopelessly in love with each new morning—that every new sunrise should hold a hidden promise in its warm glow. Maybe *you* were the wrong one for believing there could be more out there for you. But no. *No*. I promise. You weren't wrong. The part of you that believes in your unending worthiness has never been wrong. You deserve to live a life that aligns with your heart and feeds your soul—a life that feels *right* and *real* and *true* to you. The time for settling is over. That's in the past. Because my goodness, you are worth so much more than a life you settle for. You are not here to settle. You are here to *create* and *explore* and follow the pull inside your heart just to see where it takes you. You are here to leave the world a little more beautiful than you found it. You are here to breathe into the infinite possibilities of a limitless universe. Don't settle. Never settle. You are worth so much more.

You have this way about you. This effortless charisma that you don't even know you have. You're not a passing fad or fading trend. You're as timeless as the morning sunrise. As irreplaceable as the moon that holds this earth in place. And would you really trade that all in for a temporary high? For a quick fix? For a dose of counterfeit acceptance based on a cardboard cutout you think you need to pretend to be. Would you really waste your beautiful uniqueness on something so flimsy and insubstantial? Is it really worth it? Knowing that your wild heart is unmatched and priceless—could you really put your originality up for sale? Nobody like you has ever existed before. Nobody like you will ever exist again. And to think—you have a chance to offer something to the world that you and only you can give. You can breathe life into the stagnant air with your words and thoughts and ideas—with the way you think and speak and move. You can rise above the sea of echoes and create something lasting and eternal. That's your power.

You are not them. You are you. You have gifts that can't be duplicated. You have your own luminous glow. You are irreplaceable. Priceless. Beyond comparison. But still, you do it—compare yourself to people who have something that you think you don't. You compare yourself in your mind so that *they* always come out better and *you* are always worse. And there are days when you wish you could alter the core of who you are to be more like them. Funnier. Smarter. More confident and charismatic. Someone captivating. *Someone who lights up a room.* But can't you see? You carry a spark inside you that has the power to radiate outward and illuminate every space you walk through. You possess a magnetic pull that grows stronger when you honor your unique originality and allow your true self to be seen. You have a quiet power that effortlessly draws in the right people and things and experiences. Who you are is exactly right. But it doesn't matter if the rest of the world believes it. You need to believe it. You have to know in your *body* and *breath* and *every cell of your being* that you are not too much or not enough of anything. And I hope one day you see that not being them—*being you*—that's your gift.

How long will you keep doubting yourself before you realize your potential is *limitless*? How long will you keep devaluing your worth before you realize that you are *priceless*? How long will you keep minimizing the importance of your dreams before you realize that your dreams have a *place* and *purpose* in this world? How long will you keep looking for answers outside yourself before you realize the guidance you're seeking is *within you*? How long will you keep trusting only what your eyes can see before you realize the truth exists *inside your heart*? How long will you keep playing small before you realize you're meant for *so much more*? How long will you keep hiding your true self before you realize this world *desperately* wants to see you shine? How long will you keep waiting? How long will you keep holding back? And how long will you keep chasing the sun before you realize the sun is *inside you*?

I hope you know that you have nothing to prove. I know it doesn't always feel that way. I know how easy it is to get wrapped up in other people's opinions. And even when you try not to, you fall into the trap of tying your worth to your achievements like a packed resumé is proof that you're something special. And it feels like you need to show people—*See what I can do? Do you see that I'm enough? Can you see my worth and usefulness?* But you don't actually need to prove anything. You don't need to show people that you're important. Outward success doesn't make you more worthy of someone's energy. You're already worthy of love and respect and acceptance and everything good in this world. And I hope whatever path you choose in life, you don't choose it solely to prove something. Because there's no end to that path. There's no peace down that road. And I promise—you're already so incredibly worthy and important and needed. You've spent enough time trying to prove your worth. Let this next chapter be written with your worthiness already tied to every single word.

We watch the sunrise and gaze at the starry skies from our backyards and think, *this is a perfect creation.* We stand with our feet in the sand and look out upon the ocean and think, *this has to be proof that there's something greater at work in this universe.* We hold our breath as we scroll through images of galaxies from space telescopes and marvel at the magnificence of life's creation. We find perfection in the world all around us. And yet, we convince our minds that we ourselves are somehow inherently wrong. We tell ourselves that we are imperfect. A mistake. We can't let ourselves believe that the same force that created the oceans and galaxies could possibly have crafted us with the same care as well. We can praise the majesty of the earth and moon but can't fathom that this same splendor exists in our own beings. We find beauty even in nature's imperfections but not in our own. But do you really think the beauty you see in the world outside yourself isn't a reflection of what's inside you? Do you really believe you're not as luminous as all those distant galaxies? Do you really think that the same force that gifted the earth with ocean waves and wildflowers didn't believe that you were a gift, too?

When you see something beautiful in the universe, know that it's a reflection of what's inside you. And when you see something that takes your breath away, know that this same energy exists within you. And when you watch the world in wonder and gaze at the awe-inspiring gifts that fill the world, know that you, yourself, are a gift, too.

The greatest love story ever told can't be found in the pages of a book or the fleeting images on a movie screen. There aren't pages of fanfiction dedicated to its existence. Most of the time, it passes by quietly, barely mentioned. Often overlooked. But still—there is hope and heartache, grief and pain. And in the end, a love that stands the test of time. The greatest love story ever told is the story you're writing right now. The story of how you fell deeply and unconditionally in love with the truth of who you are. It's the story of how you stripped away expectations of who you thought you were supposed to be and sank deeper into your true and authentic self. The greatest love story ever told is the story of how you fell hopelessly in love with the sacred stardust that created you. With the magic that lives within you. And with the everlasting light that shines like the night sky through every single cracked and broken fragment inside your being.

It's not your clothes or the way you style your hair. It's not your weight or body type. It's not the shape of your nose or the color of your eyes. No—that's not why they fall in love with you. They fall in love with your heart. Your energy. With the way you make them see the world in a way they never have before. They fall in love with your irrepressible spirit and the kindness you radiate out into the universe. They fall in love with your bravery. How you keep putting yourself out there, even when it's scary. How you don't hide in the shadows of life but walk fully in the light. And if there is no light, you're willing to share yours—you give it away freely without ever asking for anything in return. Can't you see? It's who you are at your core. That mind that always looks for the good. That heart that keeps beating through the joy and the pain. *It's the way you make them feel.* That's what they love. That's what's sacred. It's the beauty that radiates from within—your true essence. *The magic that you don't even know you carry.* It's you, exactly as you are. You are worth loving. You are worth cherishing. You are worth everything.

PART 2: THIS IS FOR RECONNECTING WITH YOUR DREAMS

What would you do today if you knew that the gifts you possess inside yourself are exactly what this world needs? What steps would you take if you knew that everything you are is everything that someone else out there is looking for? How brave would you be if you knew that you could heal with the power of your words, your art, your energy, your presence? What choices would you make if you knew that you already have what it takes to be extraordinary? And what would you do if you knew that nothing about you is a mistake? That there is a divine purpose to every single part of you? That you are so much more than you've ever given yourself credit for? Would you share your gifts if you knew they could change the world? That they could change just one person's world? That they matter. That they're needed. That they're so much more valuable than you've ever realized.

Would you share your words if you knew there's a person out there who needs to hear exactly what you have to say? Would you display your art if you knew it had the power to heal and spark inspiration in another? Would you choose to be a coach or mentor if you knew that the skills and knowledge you possess could profoundly transform someone's life for the better? Would you offer your unique gifts if you knew that they could change the world? That they could change just one person's world? That everything you possess is everything someone else out there is waiting for. Will you be brave for that one person? That one person who needs what you can offer. That one person who is searching for your words, your art, your guidance, your wisdom, *that thing that only you have.* Can you do it for that one person? That one person who needs to hear your story. Who needs to experience your light. That one person who needs the spark of magic that you carry. Can you trust that who you are and what you possess inside you is more than enough? Are you willing to step forward and offer the thing only *you* can give?

Get it out of your head and into the world. Your art. Your ideas. Your creations. The music that only you can hear. The stories that only you can tell. The creativity that flows through your body like it's as much a part of you as your *blood* and your *breath* and your *bones*. Don't ask if it's good. Ask if it's true. Ask if it means something. Ask if it makes you laugh or cry or dance or scream—if it makes you feel. Because God knows if you have the power to create something that can break through the numbness and make a person feel—that's what we need more of in this world. I don't care if your voice is shaky or your lines are crooked or your commas are out of place. I care that this thing you've shared with me gives me a glimpse of humanity and rattles my insides and shows me the world through eyes I haven't looked through before. If you have that inside you, then please—*pour it out.*

Please—if there's something you want to make, *make it*. The art. The music. The poetry that swirls through your mind in the middle of the night. Get it out of your body and into the world. Whatever it is that interests you, that fascinates you, that makes you feel alive—*go there*. Don't keep these treasures buried inside you because you worry about what other people will think. Life's too short. It goes by too fast. And there's so little time for us all here—don't spend it fiercely clinging onto your magic like you'll lose it if you let it out. You won't lose it. Energy flows and ideas multiply and the magic keeps growing the more you set it free. If it makes your heart beat faster, if it gets you excited, if it makes you *feel*—then please, give the world a chance to feel it, too. Don't deny your gifts. Your talents. Your passions. Don't deny what enchants and excites you. Don't bury it inside yourself because you worry it's not good enough. It's enough. You're enough. If you can do only one thing for yourself—*just give yourself a chance*.

The question isn't, *is it enough for them?* The question is, *is it enough for you?* Create something you love. Build something you've been dreaming about. Write something that excites you. Is there something you wish there were more of in the world? *Make it.* Paint with the colors that call to you. Write the novel that you want to read. Record the podcast that you want to listen to. Create the program that you want to purchase. Produce the music that vibrates deep within your bones and sticks with you long after the melody has faded. Focus on what *you* love. On what brings you joy. On what lights up your heart—even when it isn't the thing everyone else is doing. Especially when it isn't the thing everyone else is doing. That's how you create greatness. That's how you make something meaningful that leaves a lasting impact on the world. Not by trying to be enough for everyone else but by being enough for yourself.

When you're uncertain of your purpose in this world, look for the places where your love is needed most. *How can I offer love today? Where is love missing? Where are the gaps? The holes? What can I give to fill the empty spaces? Where is my presence most needed?* We all have our own unique ways of offering love. Maybe it's in the art you create. Maybe it's in the words you speak. Maybe it's in the way you show up— how you offer your time and energy to something bigger than yourself. How you make people feel seen. Maybe it's in your advocacy. Your knowledge. Your mentorship and guidance. Or maybe it's in the food you cook. The photos you take. The stories you write. That thing you *make, build, create, do, arrange, produce, organize,* and *share.* There are infinite ways you can offer love today. Keep looking for the places where your love is needed most. Because right there—that's where your purpose lives.

You have what it takes to be extraordinarily successful. Your mind is brilliant. Your heart is strong. You have so much to offer—more than you even realize. Nobody else in the world has the unique combination of talents, abilities, and life experiences that you have. Nobody. Every dream that's been placed in your heart is there for a reason. Nothing is by accident. Nothing is by mistake. Stop telling yourself that this dream you have is only meant for an elite class of really special people that you're not a part of—that it's for everyone but you. Trust that if something ignites a fire in your soul, it's because it's meant for you. Love your dream. Protect it. Believe in it. Open yourself up to receiving a lifetime of beautiful and soul-enriching experiences. Because this dream was meant for a person exactly like you.

People have been calling you *stubborn* your entire life like it's a bad thing. They weaponize the word against you like your strong will is somehow wrong. But nothing about you is wrong. Your stubbornness? It's a gift. This world was *built* on the shoulders of stubborn hearts. Your stubbornness means you don't just have dreams and visions—you also have the persistence to make them come true. Your stubbornness isn't rigidity. It's not ignoring what's there and only seeing what you want to see. No—it's seeing what's there and asking, *"How can I make this work for me?"* Your stubbornness means you'll never give up on the things that mean something. The things that matter. People. Beliefs. Dreams. And most of all, yourself. And at the end of the day, when everyone else has lost hope, you'll still hold strong. You're the undying flame this world so badly needs. So never let anyone tell you that your stubbornness is a flaw. The stubborn heart beating inside your chest is going to change this world.

The greatest gift you can offer the world is your truest, most authentic self. You were created exactly as you are because who you are is who this world needs. It's your kindness. Your humor. Your passion. Your originality. It's the fire that burns inside you. It's your fierce courage and irrepressible spirit. It's the way you love with your whole entire being—fully, unapologetically, no holding back. It's your unique presence. Your divine signature. It's the way your smile can change a person's entire day. How your heart pours out love without expectations or conditions. It's the wisdom that lives inside you. Your voice. Your words. Your ideas. Your unique way of seeing the world. You're an original. Unmatched. Incomparable. Second to none. Let go of who you think you're supposed to be and step into your truest self. Be who you are. Offer what only you can give. You will never be *too much* or *not enough* for the people worthy of experiencing the fullest expression of you.

If you look for reasons why you can't, you'll find them. That's the easy part. Your mind is tuned into self-protection. It'll search for all the ways it can keep you safe. Safe from failure. Safe from rejection. Safe from ever experiencing the pain that comes with trying something and having it not work out the way you hoped. But there comes a day when you realize that what once felt safe is now holding you back. That maybe you need to reframe your perspective. That maybe it's time to start telling a new story—a story of why you can. *I can because I'm so much stronger than I realize. I can because there's an untapped fountain of potential inside me that can take me further than I've ever imagined. I can because I'm talented and capable and competent. I can because the universe is always supporting me. I can because I trust myself.* Your power is in your perspective. It's in the stories you tell. In the thoughts you focus on. And all that matters—all that has ever mattered—is what you choose to believe.

Actually, you can. You can follow your heart. You can alter your path. You can break the mold. You can take the leap. You can free yourself from your fears. You can refuse to settle for less than you deserve. You can live a life aligned with your purpose and passions. You can do the thing you're not sure you can do. You can take the first step. You can create your future. You can have *exactly* what you've been dreaming about. You are strong enough. You are brave enough. You have what it takes.

Your future is in your own hands. Where you go, what you do, how you live your life—it's all up to you. Instead of focusing on what you can't control, focus on what you can. Maybe you can't go back and change your past choices. You can't recreate your history. You can't redetermine the outcomes that led you down this path. But today, right now, in this moment, you can choose how you show up for yourself. You can choose how you respond to the world around you. You can choose what you want in life, and you can also choose whether or not you'll go for it. You get to choose your next step. You get to choose how you respond to the obstacles and challenges on your path. You get to choose whether you'll let the universe surprise you with its magic. And you get to choose whether you lean into faith or fear, trust or doubt, hope or despair. You have so much more power than you think. You have the ability to create the life that calls to you. The life your heart's being pulled to. The life that feels like it's already yours. You have the tools. The resources. The support of an infinite universe that wants to see you succeed. Now what you do with the time you have left is all up to you.

You *can*, and it doesn't take any special superpowers or secret knowledge that you don't already have. Are you willing to show up for yourself? Can you remain steady and consistent? Can you encounter challenges with an open mindset and a readiness to learn? When roadblocks prevent you from proceeding down the path you're on, are you able to step back and get a wider perspective—to let these obstacles be redirections to previously unseen possibilities? Are you willing to trust yourself? Can you separate your worthiness from your achievements, knowing that nothing outside of you can ever lessen the importance of your existence? Can you let every breakdown break you open instead of shutting you closed? And can your greatest superpower be your own steady heart and unwavering self-belief?

Next time someone accuses you of having your head in the clouds, tell them it's your favorite place to be. When someone calls you a dreamer, tell them you're a visionary. When someone says you need to be more realistic, let them know you create your own reality. When someone insists it's impractical, respond, *"But not impossible."* When someone claims it's wishful thinking, remind them that all the great innovators and creators were once just wishful thinkers, too. When someone says you're mad for trying, tell them there's magic in the madness. When someone tells you it'll never work, remind them that you'll never know unless you try. When someone asks what you'll do if you fail, tell them you don't fear failure. You only fear never trying. Always wondering. Never knowing what could've been.

You're a dreamer, but you don't stop at just dreaming. You're a dreamer *and* a doer. You visualize the truest, most beautiful life you can imagine for yourself, and then you take inspired action to create this vision in your reality. You understand that adversity is part of the process, but you don't fear it because you know something that so many people miss: hardship, adversity, failure—it's never the end unless you allow it to be. And when people tell you that your dreams aren't practical, you don't get angry. You're steady. Centered. Unshaken. You're a visionary. A creator. An innovator. Even though your head may be in the clouds sometimes, your feet are always rooted to the ground. And you don't need to convince anyone else of what you feel deep inside because you know in your heart what's right. And that's all the validation you need to keep going. To keep rising. To keep living with your heart wide open. To never stop walking toward your dreams.

If you're still thinking about it after all this time, maybe that means you should just go for it. Start the business. Write the book. Travel the world. Follow your heart. Do what you love. Imagine yourself in the future looking back on your life, and if there's a single thing that would cause your future self to think, *"I wish I would've done that,"* then you owe it to yourself to do that thing. Jump out of a plane. Swim in the ocean. Book the trip. Take the class. *Say yes to what you really want.* The years are going to pass by so fast. There's no time for lingering regrets and *what ifs*. So maybe you should do it. The thing your heart is pulling you towards. The thing you think about when you lie awake at night. *The thing you can't get out of your head.* Take a chance on life. Go all in on yourself. Pour your whole heart into the act of living.

Don't do it for validation. Don't do it for recognition or applause. Don't do it to prove yourself to someone who didn't believe in you. Don't do it because you think you need to demonstrate your worth. And don't do it because you think success is how you earn love—because maybe if you succeed in this one thing, maybe then they'll notice you. Maybe then you'll be important. *No.* You have nothing to prove. Don't do it for them. Do it for *you.* Do it because you love it. Because you can't stop thinking about it. Because every cell in your body is gently whispering, *go here.* Do it because it fills you with genuine excitement. Because you care about it too deeply to give up. Do it because it *adds* to your life more than it takes. Do it because the sacrifice it requires doesn't feel like sacrifice at all—it feels like *alignment.* Do it because it makes you feel alive. Because it adds colors to your life you didn't know existed. Because it lights up your soul and fills you with *passion* and *purpose.* Do it because your heart beats for it. Because it feels good. Because it feels right. Do it because you have something important to offer the world. Something that matters. Do it to serve. To inspire. Do it to be the light that this world needs.

What's impossible for *them* doesn't have to be impossible for *you*. What limits *them* doesn't have to limit *you*. And what stops *them* from going after what they truly want in life doesn't have to stop *you*. You get to decide your limits. You get to decide how far you can go. You get to decide what you're capable of achieving. And you get to decide just how much you're willing to believe in yourself. This story is yours and yours alone, so don't borrow someone else's beliefs about what's possible and let *their* words fill *your* pages. You are the sole guardian, protector, and keeper of your dreams, and you're the only one who can decide how far you're willing to follow them. You're the only one who can decide what's worth fighting for. You're the only one who can decide whether or not you'll believe. So don't look at *them* for proof of what is and isn't possible. Look inside yourself. Listen to that inner voice. What does your heart tell you?

You're the author of your success story. Not *them*. So don't let other people's lack of belief influence *your* next chapter. Everything was impossible until it wasn't. Everything was unimaginable until someone dared to imagine it. Everywhere you look, you're surrounded by ideas and things that didn't exist until someone decided to create it. Whatever you decide you can and can't do—don't base it on what other people tell you. Write your own narrative. Trust your own instincts. Make your own path. Maybe it's impossible for them, but it doesn't have to be impossible for you.

And maybe *impossible* is just a synonym for *hasn't been done yet*. Maybe *unimaginable* means that you just have to stretch your imagination a little bit further. Maybe *illogical* means that logic simply doesn't play a role in this story—that instead of leading with your head this time, it's your heart that knows the way. Maybe when the odds are stacked against you, that's when you have the highest potential to rise. Maybe when you're afraid of what you might lose, you simply can't see what you're about to gain. Maybe when the path ahead is unknown, that means you're moving in the right direction. Maybe when you're uncertain about what's going to happen, that means anything is still possible. And maybe the old rules were always meant to be broken and limits were always meant to be pushed. And maybe if you can't get it out of your head, that's your sign that you should take the risk.

Why not you? Why can't you be the one who succeeds? What's stopping you from stepping forward into your passion and purpose? If worthiness is a question, you're already wildly worthy. If it's a matter of *how*, know that you don't need to see the whole path right now to begin—you only need your intuition to guide you forward, one small step at a time. And if you're worried about failing, remember that failure isn't the worst thing in the universe anyway. And for every so-called failure, more doors will open. More opportunities will come. You just have to give yourself a chance. So the only thing that's standing in your way now is *belief*. Are you willing to believe in yourself? Can you believe that you've been given this dream for a reason? Will you allow yourself to believe that you were born for this? History is filled with people who started with nothing *but* belief. So why not you?

They are not braver than you. *They* are not more capable than you. *They* are not luckier than you. And *they* are absolutely not more worthy than you. There is nothing that *they* have that you can't have, too. The only force in the world that can stop you is *you*. Are you willing to believe in yourself enough to be brave? To take a chance? To do something you've never done before? Are you willing to stand in your undeniable worthiness and declare that you'll no longer settle for less than you deserve? Are you willing to step out of a comfort zone that stopped feeling comfortable a long time ago? Are you willing to own your story? To walk your authentic path? To keep going in the face of obstacles and uncertainty? Are you willing to fail? To pick yourself back up? To learn from your mistakes? Are you willing to try? To grow? To expand? To live?

Do you know how many people have built empires from nothing but their own self-belief? Do you know how many people have gone further than they ever dared to dream simply because they decided to give themselves a chance? Do you know how many people have found their wings and soared simply because they refused to listen to the voices that told them it was impossible? They didn't have anything you don't have. They didn't have directions, and they couldn't see the entire path ahead. All they had was a vision and a feeling that they had to do this—that if they didn't, they'd regret it for the rest of their lives. They took one step at a time and trusted that they'd figure it out. And that's it. That's the secret to success that everyone is always searching for. We complicate it with our overthinking minds, but it's the simplest formula in the world that works time and time again: self-trust, an open mind, and a willingness to try. So what's the thing you're going to keep thinking about for the rest of your life? *Go that way.* Maybe it'll work out exactly as you imagine, or maybe there's something else waiting for you at the end of that path. But either way, it's worth taking the chance.

It's not about what you *should* do. Who you *should* be. How you *should* feel. *Should* is not the answer—not when it feels like it's pulling you further away from yourself. *I should stick with what I know. I should stay in my lane. I should be what everyone else wants me to be. I should do the safe thing.* Don't let *should* keep you from following your authentic path. Don't let it stop you from staying true to yourself. Don't *should* yourself out of the life you envision when you close your eyes. How *do* you feel? What *do* you want? Where do you see yourself in the future? *Who are you at your core?* Dig in. Go deeper. Pour yourself into all that you are. Don't build your life on a foundation of *shoulds*. There is no *should*. There is only you and your beating heart and what feels *right* and *real* in every cell of your being.

Never let anyone sell you on the secret to a lifetime of happiness and fulfillment if that so-called secret is something that exists outside yourself. The secret isn't *out there*. It's never been out of reach. The secret has always been *right here*. Within you. All around you. *Begging to be noticed*. The secret is expressing from the heart. Creating from the heart. Communicating from the heart. *Living from the heart*. The secret is having the courage to step out of the mundane, the soul-numbing, the *never-ending cycles* we trap ourselves in as we convince ourselves that this *emptiness we feel* is the way it's *supposed to be*. Yes, our thinking minds are important, but we've prioritized them to the detriment of our heart's wisdom. If you're looking for the secret thing to change your life, it's right here inside you. Waiting. Wishing. *Hoping you'll notice*. Can you live from the heart today? Can you speak from the heart? Can you uncover the truth that only reveals itself when you go within? Can you trust that this pull inside your heart may be exactly the thing you've been searching for? Do you have the courage to follow your heart and find out where it leads?

In the end, the one piece of guidance that matters is this: stay true to yourself. That's all we can ever do here. There are thousands of writers and coaches and podcast hosts—millions of experts who can try to tell you how to live and think and *be*. Some will resonate. Some won't. It doesn't mean any of them are right or wrong—it's just a matter of what feels right to you. It's true that what's meant for you won't pass you by, but the road you travel on looks and feels different when you remain aligned with your authentic self. And this doesn't mean it will always be easy. No—staying true to yourself often requires you to do the hard thing. To make tough choices. To follow the uncertain path that doesn't make sense to the rational mind but feels right and real to the beating heart. If there's only one piece of wisdom you carry with you throughout your life, let it be this: stay true to yourself, always. When you're creating. When you're deciding. When you're communicating. When you're *living*. Don't abandon yourself for anything or anyone.

You make the world better simply by showing up as your wholehearted, imperfect, authentic self. *Your presence is a gift.* When you stay true to yourself, you give other people the courage to stay true to themselves, too. And if there's anything this world needs more of, it's more acceptance. More honest connections. More open hearts and authenticity. So if you can let go of any stories you're carrying about who you *should be* and just embody who you truly are, you're doing so much more than you'll ever realize. But then—if you have it in you to do just *a little bit more*—please, follow your heart. Embrace your dreams. Cultivate your gift. And when you feel called to—share it. Offer it. Give it away. Don't worry if it's enough. I promise, it is. There will be people who love your vibe. There will be people who need what you have to offer. There will be people who feel inspired by you. People who feel drawn to you. And there will be people who will feel grateful for your existence. People who don't know how they would've made it without you. These are your people. Give them a chance to find you.

Every day, you make a difference. You make a difference in the way you interact with the world. How you treat others. The example you set. You make a difference in ways you can't see—words you say that stick with another person for years. Actions that have a rippling effect far beyond your scope of vision. You make a difference when you allow yourself to be seen. When you step out of the shadows and shine your light. You make a difference when you show up, afraid and uncertain but ready and willing to be brave. You make a difference, whether purposeful or not. Whether you want to or you don't. You can't hide from the power you possess to make an impact on the world. But it's up to you to decide how you'll use that power. What kind of legacy you'll leave behind. It's up to you to decide what kind of difference you want to make.

Can't you see? Life wants to move through you. To work with you. To show you the magic that spills from your fingertips. Life is on your side. It shows up in tiny miracles and unexplainable synchronicities. In that soft whisper you hear deep inside yourself. In gentle nudges and magnetic pulls that draw you forward—to places you've never been. To unknown paths. To a future filled with uncertainty but also brimming with possibilities. It shows up in the signs you see everywhere you look. In that song you keep hearing. That message you keep seeing. Those words you can't get out of your head. It shows up in your heart's wisdom. In that feeling that doesn't make sense that keeps calling to you. That beckons you forward. That guides you on a path that only you can travel. Life doesn't require perfection. It just asks for your trust. Trust that what you're seeing, what you're hearing, what you're feeling deep inside yourself—it's all on purpose. It's all part of life force energy. Working through you. With you. For you. Always.

You can love your life deeply and appreciate all that you have and still honor the voice within telling you there's something *more* out there for you. Honoring your dreams doesn't lessen the life you have now, just like loving your life now doesn't lessen the beauty of your dreams. You have unconditional permission to do both: to fall in love with your life in this moment, exactly as it is, while listening to that inner voice that tells you there's something *more.*

There's this one life. This one life where you get to choose where you go and what you do and who you get to be. You get to choose your mindset. Your actions. Your reactions. You get to choose your attitude and perceptions. You get to choose what you *say* and *do* and *think*. You have the power every single day. And whatever you choose—I hope you honor your inner wisdom and make brave choices and follow the path that feels like love and freedom and bliss. I hope you go for it. The dreams. The visions. The things that spark your inner voice to whisper, *this is right*. I hope you let go of other people's rules and stories for how you're supposed to live and learn how to trust what feels genuine deep down in your core. And I hope that if there's one thing you trust in this world, it's your heart. I hope if there's one thing you honor above all else, you honor what you feel. And if there's one thing you stay true to throughout your life, it's to the deep inner knowing that flows through your bloodstream and wraps around your bones and makes you feel vital and alive and whole. And I hope that if there's something deep within telling you *this is right* and *this is real* and *this is for me*—I hope you trust that feeling. Honor it. At the very least, please—give it a chance.

PART 3: THIS IS FOR LETTING GO

If you aren't happy with where you are in your life right now, I promise, there's somewhere better out there for you. You don't have to bloom where you're planted if the soil beneath your feet doesn't contain the nutrients you need to grow. If the space you're in doesn't feed your soul, stimulate your mind, nurture your creativity—*if it doesn't make you feel safe but still free*—then you are not required to make it work. There is still a great big world out there waiting to be explored. There are places you've never been. Experiences you've never had. And right now, you've only seen a tiny fraction of what's out there for you. You are worthy of finding your people. Finding your safety net. Finding the place that feels like home. And if you have to get lost for a little while to find it, that's okay. Sometimes, getting lost is the greatest act of self-discovery you'll ever embark upon. Let yourself get lost in the city lights and crowded streets. Get lost in the blue skies and wildflowers. Get lost in the layers of yourself that you begin to shed as you start to unearth the deepest parts of your inner being—the parts you thought were gone but were really just waiting to be reclaimed. And maybe getting lost is how you discover where you're truly meant to be. Maybe this is how you find your way.

If you're currently on a path you're no longer sure you want to be on, stepping back isn't quitting. It's *energetic alignment*. It's honoring your own inner wisdom. It's trusting your instincts. It's choosing yourself over other people's perceptions. It's giving yourself a chance to discover what you *do* want. It's being your own greatest advocate. It's standing in your power. It's self-kindness. Self-love. *Self-care*. If you're worried about losing what you've built, know that none of the time you spent on this old path has been wasted. You were meant to be here. To grow. To learn from these experiences. You're not the same person you were when you started. So give yourself permission to courageously forge your own path. Start over carrying with you the wisdom of your past experiences. Allow yourself to begin again.

All of the biggest decisions of your life will begin with the same question: *"Can I really do this?"* Don't look outside yourself for the answer. What does your heart tell you? What wisdom emerges from that quiet voice deep within? What direction is your inner guidance system pointing you towards? *How does it make you feel?* Don't wait for validation from the outside world to confirm what you already know deep inside. Trust your intuition to guide your next step. You know so much more than you think. You hold more power than you realize. *You already know what you must do because you hear the words echoing in your heart.* Do you want to carve out your own path? To create your own story? To do something you've never done before? Then don't be afraid of the wealth of wisdom that flows through every cell of your being. You have the answers. You possess the understanding. You just have to trust yourself.

It's not a mistake. Taking a chance. Starting a new path. Choosing the thing that feels right but doesn't come with any promises or guarantees. If the other choice is spending your whole life wondering what would've happened— *wishing you just would've tried*—then it's not a mistake. Sometimes, you have to believe in what you can't see but what you can feel. You have to listen to the voice that says, *this is right*. You have to trust that *you and you alone* know what's best for you—and those directions don't come from the overthinking mind but from your beating heart. There's something inside you that isn't tangible. It can't be put in a box or easily explained. But it feels. It understands. It holds the directions. It sees what your eyes can't. It knows the way. You have everything you need to navigate this path with strength and grace. And I promise, you don't have to settle for anything half-hearted. Not now. Not ever. So please know—it's not a mistake. Not if it feels right. Not if this is where your heart is calling you toward.

My future needs me. My future needs me to take care of myself. To honor my needs. To love myself enough to do what's right for me. My future needs me to be brave. To trust my strength. To walk into experiences that bring me long-term growth, even when they also bring short-term unease. My future needs me to be honest with myself. To have the hard conversations. To make the difficult choices. To see what's there and not just what I want to see. My future needs me to feel all my feelings. The heavy. The hard. *The ones that make me feel like I can't breathe.* It needs me to cry, laugh, yell, and scream. It needs me to release what needs to be released so I can make space for new energy. New experiences. New opportunities. *New possibilitie*s. And most of all, my future needs me to be here now. To show up for myself today in the small and big ways. It needs me to choose courage and compassion, honesty and love. To choose the path that feels right to me. To trust myself.

The past only knows where you've been—it doesn't know where you're going. Your past failures don't predict future failures. Past heartbreak isn't an indicator of future heartbreak. Past mistakes don't ensure future mistakes. Don't create your future from your past—create it from your *now*. Your power is in the present moment. Your power is in your vibration. Your power is in the way you show up for yourself. Your power is in the breath that flows through your lungs. Your power is in the soft yet persistent beating of your stubborn, resilient heart. It's in the quiet pauses you take throughout your day. It's in the effortless flow of energy moving through you. It's in the choices you make. It's in how you choose to view the world. The past is only a small part of your story, but you're a story in the making. Your path is still unfolding. You get to create your future from your now.

Maybe the past *you* didn't have the courage, but the present *you* does. Maybe the past *you* failed, but the present *you* can draw wisdom from those experiences in order to succeed. Maybe the past *you* was afraid, but the present *you* knows something you didn't know back then: you don't have to be fearless. You just have to be willing to feel every ounce of fear and not let it stop you from moving forward. The past *you* wasn't sure you'd bounce back from adversity, but the present *you* now knows that you're so much more resilient than you ever gave yourself credit for. The past *you* didn't know your own strength, but the present *you* has learned how to summon it time and time again. So maybe the past *you* wasn't ready. But now? The present *you* knows that this is exactly what you've been waiting for. This is your time. So go ahead—take what you need from the past and go claim your future.

You've been going back and forth for so long. Second guessing yourself. Questioning if you can really do this. Leaning into all the ways this might backfire catastrophically. But still, you can't shake the feeling that this unknown path might lead you to a place even more beautiful than you can imagine. That this is right. That this is real. And that maybe, if it's still in your mind after all this time, it's worth taking the risk. And maybe you owe it to yourself to see where this path leads. Maybe this feeling deep inside is actually your inner compass, and maybe this dream you can't stop thinking about is actually your true north. Maybe you really can do this. Maybe you don't need it to make sense to move forward. Maybe your heart knows something your eyes can't see. And maybe—maybe that's enough.

You worry about what will happen if the answer is *no*, but if you don't try, the answer will always be *no*. If you don't give yourself a chance, you'll be forever putting up walls around yourself—stopping yourself from succeeding before the world even has a chance to know you. To see you. To experience the fullest expression of all that you are. If you don't risk someone else's *no*, you'll never feel that pure exhilaration of one day hearing *yes*. Don't let the fear of rejection stop you from pursuing your dreams. Rejection is merely an experience, just like any other. And if you're willing to risk it, you might find out that it's not as bad as you think. You may even discover all the ways it can redirect you to an even better path—somewhere real. Somewhere true. To the place you were always meant to be. You don't have to be fearless of what's to come—you just have to be willing. If you want something you've never had, you have to be willing to do what you've never done. You have to be willing to hear the *no* and not let it break you. You have to be willing to put yourself out there. You have to be willing to say *yes* to yourself.

But what if you're wrong? What if all the worst-case scenarios you're constantly replaying in your mind never actually come true? What if nothing bad happens at all? What if the absolute worst possible outcome of stepping forward and trying is that you simply learn from the experience and grow through what you go through? What if the limits you've accepted aren't real? What if all the challenges you've encountered are actually part of your success story? What if the path ahead is even easier and more beautiful than you can imagine? What if you were made for so much more than you've ever dreamed? What if there's something truly incredible waiting for you on the other side of fear? What if taking this first step leads to a lifetime of true purpose and fulfillment? What if it's the best decision you ever make? What if you really can have it all? What if this is just the beginning of something extraordinary?

If you keep pushing the edges of your limits, you'll soon realize those edges only ever existed in your mind. If you confront the fears that have been holding you back, you'll discover that fear has no power without your permission. If you're brave enough to step toward what you want most in life, limitless possibilities will open up in front of you. Life shows up for you when you show up for yourself. But you have to be willing to fight for it. You have to believe that your strength is greater than any struggle. You have to trust your ability to persevere. You have to call upon your inner resilience. And you have to know in every cell of your being that *you already have what it takes*. Starting is the hardest part. And if you have the courage to begin, you have the courage to keep going. You have the courage to walk this path with faith and grace. You have the courage to rise above any challenge. And you have the courage to succeed. You just have to know in every cell of your being that *how far you go* and *what you're capable of* isn't dependent on other people—it all begins and ends with you.

Isn't it funny how every time you think, *I could never do that*, the universe leads you to exactly that thing? *I could never leave. I could never stay. I could never open up. I could never be that brave.* The truth is, the thing you think you can't do—you can. The words you're not sure you can say. The step you don't think you can take. The chance, the risk, the pull that's leading you in a different direction. You are so much stronger and more capable than you've ever realized. You can walk this path with courage and faith. You can do the hard thing. You just have to ask yourself—what's more important than fear? What's worth being brave for? And when you find that thing, hold onto it. Make your purpose bigger than your fear. Because that thing you don't think you can do? It's going to be one of the greatest things you've ever done. You're going to find out how strong you really are. You're going to learn that you are so much more than you've ever given yourself credit for. You're going to set yourself free.

All I can tell you is, it's worth it. Being brave. Putting yourself out there. Following your heart. Letting down your walls. Risking failure. Exploring new opportunities. Choosing courage over fear. Giving yourself a chance to discover what's out there in this world for you. Even the stories that don't end in happily ever after—they're still worth telling. The pain you feel as a consequence of being a tender-hearted human in a heavy world. The hope that sometimes ends in heartbreak. *The really hard parts of living.* Loving is worth it. Feeling is worth it. Trying is worth it. Not holding back. Not minimizing yourself or your dreams. Not always taking the safe and easy road when your heart is pulling you in a different direction. It's worth it. You're worth it. Time is fleeting and your energy is sacred. Don't deny yourself the chance to truly live.

What's holding you back? What's keeping you stuck? *What are you afraid of?* Are you afraid of failure? Then put yourself in a situation where you might fail. Are you afraid of rejection? Then apply for the job, ask the person out, audition for the part, submit the manuscript—risk hearing the word *no*. Are you afraid of not being good enough? Then try something new and be willing to be bad at it. Try a hundred new things and be bad at them all. Facing your fears isn't easy. It often requires deep breaths and reminding yourself over and over again that *you're going to be okay*. But when you walk toward the thing that's been holding you back, something happens. You realize that the monster you were afraid of looked a lot scarier from far away. That maybe it isn't so bad. That maybe it can't actually hurt you. That maybe, just maybe, it can actually set you free. Fear can be a barrier or a bridge, an obstacle or an opportunity, your *biggest weakness* or your *greatest strength*. In the end, what you do with it is all up to you.

What if it was your younger self whose eyes you were looking into? What would you say? Would you tell them to dream big? To keep going? That they're worthy of knowing true happiness and fulfillment? Would you encourage them to take the safe path, or would you tell them to venture down the unmapped road their heart is calling them toward? Would you want them to go out and live a full and vibrant life? Would you give them permission to fail because at least that means they're trying? Because at least that means they're not settling. Because at least that means they're *living*. Listen to the words you'd tell your younger self and let them sink into your bones. Because those words? They're still for you. You still have permission to dream big. To follow your heart's highest calling. You're still worthy of living an extraordinary life.

There comes a day when you realize that the fear never really goes away—that if you really want something, you have to be willing to do it afraid. And maybe this is the only way you ever get to discover your fullest potential. Maybe you just have to dive right in and face the thing that scares you the most. Because in the end, it's not the rejections and so-called failures that will haunt you. It will be your own potential left unexplored. So maybe you don't need to wait until you overcome your fears to take the first step forward. Maybe you just need to know there's something more important than fear. Something greater. Something worth fighting for. And maybe overcoming your fears is the least important part of your story anyway. Maybe what matters is that you're scared but still determined. Shaky but still standing. Afraid but still willing to try.

What are you pledging your loyalty to today? Every day, you have the choice. You can stay loyal to your limits. You can remain faithful to your fears. You can stay committed to all the reasons why you can't do something. And you can remain frozen in inaction, lingering in a comfort zone that stopped feeling comfortable a long time ago. But there's also another option. A harder choice. One that will require you to dig deep and push yourself further than you ever have before. You can choose to set fire to the past agreements you made with your limits and fears and start on a new path—a path where your greatest loyalty is to your own beating heart and the undeniable pull that draws you forward. To experiences you've never had. To places you've never been. To the unknown. You can focus your energy on your own innate and undeniable potential. You can commit yourself to the vision of the future your heart is calling you towards. The choice is always yours, regardless of what you chose yesterday. Today is a new day. A new beginning. A new opportunity to draw your battle lines and choose where your allegiance resides. So it's up to you: what are you pledging your loyalty to today?

You're loyal to your family. To your friends. To your partner. You're loyal to your team, even when they're losing. And you're loyal to your beliefs and convictions, regardless of whether they make you liked or popular. But there's another type of loyalty that can get lost in the noise: loyalty to your inner voice. To the pull of your heart. To that gentle nudge you feel deep within that quietly urges you to explore something different. Something a little scary. Something you can't stop thinking about, even when it doesn't make sense. We act like these feelings don't matter when pitted against rationality and reason, but don't you see it yet? This intuitive voice buried within you is your connection to your highest, most authentic self. To your light. To your truth. So please—when you're choosing your loyalties, don't lose yourself in the noise of the outer world. Don't cast aside what you should be protecting fiercely. Don't forget your own incredible heart.

What's scarier than making the leap? Being in the exact same place today as you were last year. Being in the exact same place next year as you are today. Comfort zones that aren't really comfortable at all. Complacency in a place that doesn't let you spread your wings to find out how high you can fly. Losing your sense of wonder. Forgetting what it feels like to hope. Disconnecting from your dreams. No longer feeling passionate about the life you're living. Giving up and always wishing you had kept going. Being stuck somewhere that doesn't serve your spirit or support your growth. Trying to fit yourself into spaces you outgrew a long time ago. Never giving yourself a chance. Never knowing how far you could've gone. Not living your life for *you*. The good news is, it's never too late. You can still make the leap and take the chance—you can still live the life your heart is calling you towards.

Don't let the fear of not being the best at something stop you from moving forward. *Best* doesn't always mean most successful. You know who is successful? Someone who begins. Someone who's willing to take one step at a time and learn along the way. Someone who practices consistency over perfection. Someone who writes down their goals and follows up with aligned action. Someone who is willing to try, even if that means stumbling and picking themselves up a few times along the way. Most people will never be the absolute best at anything. Rather than trying to be the best, be the one who shows up. Be the one who's willing to learn from your experiences. Be the one who doesn't quit when faced with adversity. Be the one willing to believe in your strength over your fears. Be the one willing to trust your inner wisdom to guide you, even if it doesn't make sense to anyone else. Pour endless grace and compassion into yourself as you figure it out. That's how you succeed. Not by being the very best today, but by being willing to step forward, even when you can't see the entire path ahead. By taking one step at a time. One breath at a time. And knowing deep inside—you already have everything you need within you.

It's not about knowing all the answers. It's about having an open mind and a readiness to learn. It's about being willing to show up imperfectly—because at least you're showing up. At least you're trying. At least you're in the game. It's about being the person in the room who's willing to raise your hand and ask the questions no one else will ask. It's about admitting you don't know if you're getting this right, but you'll keep trying to get a little bit better each day. It's about leaning into the hard thing when it'd be so easy to lean away. It's about being shaky and afraid but courageous and willing. Scared but determined. Sometimes a little lost but trusting that you can find your way. It's about stumbling at times but never staying on the ground. Being willing to get it wrong until you can get it right. Always giving it your very best shot. And most of all, it's about knowing that what you need to see this through is already inside you. That you already have what it takes. That in the end, what matters most is that you believe you can.

What if *fear* and *regret* aren't the bad guys in this story? What if, together, they create a certain kind of magic? What if you allow the only fear that fuels you to be the fear *of* regret? The fear of never trying and always wondering *what if.* The fear of not writing the book. Not swimming in the ocean. Not spilling the words that have been swirling on your tongue for so long. The fear of not living with your heart wide open. Not testing the edges of your limits. Not seeing if you can go just *a little bit* further. The fear of not breaking down the walls that have been holding you back. Not making the effort. Not giving it your best shot. The fear of not following the fire in your heart. Not moving heaven and earth for your passions. Not knowing what could've been. What if the fear of regret is exactly the spark you need to finally take the leap of faith you've been dreaming about? What if it could change *everything*?

Maybe you won't be able to protect yourself from every single *what if* in life. There may always be that thing you look back on and wonder about. That outcome that could've turned out differently if you hadn't made that one choice. That fork in the road that branched off in two completely different directions. *What if I had picked a different road? Where would I be if I had walked that other path? What would've happened if I hadn't made that one decision that led me here today?* It's okay to have these thoughts. To ask these questions. It's okay to wonder. You can visit these spaces every once in a while, but don't live there. Don't let the what ifs of yesterday stop you from living the life you have today. We can't go back. We can only move forward. And if you don't like the choices you've made in the past, maybe you can't change them. But you can be intentional with the choices you make today. Every new day is an opportunity to choose again. Don't live in the choices you made yesterday. Live for today. This moment. This breath. This heartbeat.

If you never try, you'll never know. You'll never know just how capable you are. Or how far you can go. Or how ready and willing this entire universe is to support you in every way. You'll never know your fullest potential. The heights you're capable of climbing. You'll never know *where it all would've led*. You hesitate following your heart and doing the thing you truly want to do because it's unknown. Uncertain. Risky. But maybe the unknown isn't so bad. And maybe uncertainty is a gift. Maybe uncertainty is actually a synonym for *possibility*. And when you step forward and follow the path your heart is pulling you towards, infinite possibilities open up before you—endless opportunities to grow, transform, expand, receive, have, be, and succeed. So maybe the unknown path in front of you isn't so scary. Maybe it's filled with possibilities. And maybe if it's still in your mind after all this time, it's worth seeing where it leads.

I would rather fail spectacularly at doing *something* than fail quietly because I never did *anything*. I would rather fail *while* being brave than fail *at* being brave. And maybe I'll make a thousand mistakes that I'll one day laugh at and learn from, but at least I'm out here trying. At least I'm in the game. Because I know if I was sitting on the sidelines, I'd spend my whole life desperately wishing I was on the field. And I'd regret being so afraid of failure that I never gave myself a chance to succeed. I'd regret never reaching the edges of my limits so I could try to push them just a little bit further. I'd regret not exploring all of the incredible potential inside me. And more than anything, I'd regret not giving my life *all that I have*. So maybe it won't work out the way I want, but I know that no matter where this path takes me, I'll find my way. Because I trust my judgment. I trust my resilience. I trust my strength. And I trust that no matter what happens—I'll be okay.

What are we doing here if we're not creating the most beautiful lives we can imagine for ourselves? What are we doing here if we're not pouring our whole hearts into the art of magical, messy, imperfect living? What are we doing if we're not sharing our gifts? If we're not exploring our potential? What are we doing here if we're so worried about making mistakes that *we don't even try*? So please— make mistakes. Make so many mistakes. Explore the endless possibilities this world has to offer. Don't settle for a life that dulls the fire inside your heart. Don't say yes to something that slowly dims the flames burning inside you. Don't let your passions die away for the sake of just getting by. Don't let your hope wither. Don't let your light fade out. Don't accept a life only *half lived*. Can't you see? These dreams you have. These visions you can't let go of. The unshakeable feeling of *something more*. This is your calling. Your rightful path. *This is what you're here for.*

And one day, you realize that the life you're living isn't a dress rehearsal. There is no living for tomorrow. There's only today. This moment. *Right now.* And that's when you decide that you can no longer spend another day minimizing yourself, denying your dreams, or settling for less than you deserve. You can no longer let fear stop you from moving forward. You can no longer accept anything less than a life you're completely, irrevocably, head over heels in love with. And from now on, you're going to live with your heart wide open and your eyes always pointed forward. You're going to be unapologetic in the pursuit of creating a life that feels good from the inside out. You're going to fearlessly follow the call of your soul. You're going to love your life so much that you're willing to fight for it. And you're going to honor what feels right to you, even when it doesn't make sense to anyone else. You're not simply going to exist in your life—you're going to choose it. Today. Tomorrow. Always.

And what I've learned throughout my life is that the right path is probably the one that scares me. It's probably the one I keep eyeing from a distance. Wondering what would happen if I actually took that first terrifying step. What I've learned is that the more I try to ignore it, the stronger its presence. And eventually, I won't be able to avoid it. I'll have to make a choice. And my mind will come up with a million logical reasons why I shouldn't take it. It's too uncertain. Too unknown. Too risky. But my heart—all it needs is one. One reason to finally nudge me forward. One reason that matters more than any other. *Because this is right.* And what I've learned is that the right path is probably the one that has the potential to break my heart in ways that feel devastating to imagine. But if I trust myself and trust what I feel deep inside—this intangible feeling that can't be explained or understood, this deep inner knowing that says *this is for me*—then I'll be okay. And what I've learned throughout my life is that despite the fear that causes my hands to shake and my knees to tremble as I finally take that first step—it's worth it. And whether this leads exactly where I'm hoping or goes somewhere I can't imagine right now, I know that in the end, I'll be glad I came.

PART 4: THIS IS FOR MOVING FORWARD

You'll know it's meant for you when the idea of never even trying scares you more than the fear that you might fail. When you realize there's something more important than your fears. Something greater. Something that can't be ignored. You'll know it's meant for you when it feels like it isn't just something you *can* do but something you *must* do. When you've tried ignoring the call but it only gets louder. When you recognize that this gift you've been given can no longer be kept inside you—that you must share it with something bigger and greater than yourself because *this is what the world needs*. You'll know it's meant for you because every cell of your being will scream while your inner voice whispers: *This is right. This is worth it. This is the way.*

Everyone tells you that you should just begin—that if you're always waiting for the perfect time, you'll be waiting for the rest of your life. But maybe it's more than that. Maybe it's about telling yourself that it's *always* the perfect time. That every breath offers a chance for a new beginning. That this moment is the very best moment. And every new day is exactly the day you've been waiting for. Maybe it's about believing that each passing second is an irresistible opportunity to do exactly what you've been dreaming about. That there are no bad moments. There is no wrong time. There is only *right now* and the breath that flows through your body. There is only *today* and the heart beating steadily inside your chest. And maybe this day is the very best day to do exactly what you want to do. Maybe this time, it's the perfect time. To step forward. To begin. To live.

Every biggest decision of your life begins with uncertainty. Every extraordinary moment of courage comes after an internal struggle between wanting to turn back and knowing you must move forward. Every big leap comes right after a deep breath and the one question that only your heart can answer: *"Can I really do this?"* And in those moments, you will never feel ready. You will never receive all the guarantees you're looking for. There will never be absolute certainty. And you'll never be able to see all the obstacles on your path before you begin. You only ever have *right now* and a pull in your heart that can't be ignored. There is only ever this unexplainable feeling within telling you, *go this way*. There is only your inner knowing guiding you forward, one small step at a time. There is only your courage, faith, and enduring self-belief. But these *onlys*? They're not onlys at all. They're everything.

Be brave enough to take that first step. Have the courage to show up, even if you don't feel ready. Show up imperfectly. Make mistakes. Do it wrong the first time. Give yourself permission to stumble. Find lessons in your losses and opportunities in your failures. Tiptoe gently when you must. Sprint forward when it feels right. Do it for you—because every beat of your heart is calling you in this direction. Because every cell inside your body is lighting up in excitement. Because every part of you knows *this is the way*. Do it wrong until you can do it right. Do your best until you learn how to do it better. Follow the nudges. Trust the journey. Release perfection. Be brave enough to try.

This is what you do: you begin by taking one tiny step out of your comfort zone. You send the email. You submit the application. You find the one small thing that you can do today, and then you do that thing—whatever it is. However minuscule it feels. You do it when it isn't glamorous, when nobody else is around, when you get no recognition or applause. Then, you pause and breathe. You gather your strength. And you find the next small thing. You take the next tiny step. You keep moving forward— slowly, if you must. A little faster when it feels right. But always putting one foot in front of the other. And when you wake up each day, you ask yourself, what's your highest potential? Where's the furthest you can see yourself going? Just how high can you fly? And when you find the answer, you say *yes* to it. You say *yes* to being an adventurer in your own life. You say *yes* to your dreams, to your vision, to the unexplainable pull deep inside yourself. And you keep moving forward. With small steps. With deep breaths. With courage and heart and unwavering inner strength that can carry you as far as you're willing to go.

What if today is the day? The day you send the email. The day you sign up for the class. The day you submit the application. The day you start a new habit. The day you quit an old one. What if today is the day you take your daily walk in a different direction? What if today is the day you do the one thing you've been putting off—the one thing that scares you but could also set you free? What if you allowed yourself to see today through new eyes? What if today is the day you followed the pull in your heart guiding you forward? What if today, you let one thing fall apart so another thing can come together? And what if today is the day you finally receive the miracle you've been waiting for? What if it all changes today simply because you had the courage to try? What if today is the day? The day you begin. The day you start anew. The day you create something extraordinary.

It just takes one small step in the right direction to profoundly change your life forever. One small moment of courage can show you that your fears were never as scary as you once believed. One tiny spark of hope can set in motion the beginning of something extraordinary. Your life isn't defined solely by the bold jumps and daring leaps. Sometimes, it's the small moments of courage—*the things that nobody sees*—that can make the biggest impact on your future. Take one small step today. Take one more small step tomorrow. Show up for yourself, even when nobody's watching. Even when it isn't easy. Even when you have no reassurance that you'll succeed. Follow your authentic path. Honor the pull in your heart guiding you forward. And trust that your hard work is paying off in ways you can't yet see.

Yes, you'll probably be bad at it at first. That's the beauty of being a beginner—you *get* to be bad. Your first draft will be your worst. Your first audition might be a bust. Your voice might shake through that first podcast you record. And on your first day at the gym, you might only be able to lift the lightest weights. But then you write your second draft. You go on another audition. You record another podcast. You keep showing up for yourself, over and over again. You take what you learned from past efforts and carry the lessons with you the next time. And you get *a little bit better* in tiny increments. Soon, you've done it a hundred times, and you'll feel grateful that you had the courage to take that first shaky step so long ago. So never be afraid to be a beginner at something new. Be willing to be bad. Do it wrong until you finally get it right. Make a mess on the blank canvas in front of you. The mess isn't the important part. The important part is that you started. The important part is that you're here—imperfect and shaky but willing to step forward and try. And that's what will make all the difference.

The greatest gift you can give yourself is unconditional permission to fail. Let down your walls. Unguard your heart. If a possibility excites you, don't leave it unexplored. The limitless world is at your fingertips. Walk straight into it with your heart wide open. Be willing to fail spectacularly. Be willing to succeed spectacularly, too. Give life a chance to break your heart—if only to realize, most of the time, it's going to lift you so much higher than you ever dreamed of flying. If only to realize, you are so much stronger than you believed. If only to realize, you were always meant to expand further than you ever thought you could. Don't let your potential go undiscovered. Don't let the promises you've made to yourself go unfulfilled. Have courage. Have faith. Walk into the life your heart is guiding you towards.

Follow the energy. Follow the excitement. Follow the pull of your wild heart. Go toward the place where you come alive. Pursue the breadcrumbs your daydreams leave behind—the things you can't stop thinking about when you close your eyes. Flow with the rhythm of your inner music. Go after the goosebumps and butterflies and good vibes. Travel toward your unexplored potential. Seek out the people and places that feel like *love* and *freedom* and *truth*. You don't need a map or guidebook to show you the way. Listen to your inner guidance system. Trust the energy. Notice the vibration—how does it make you feel? Go toward the love. The joy. The peace. The fulfillment. Follow the alignment. Pay attention to what feels forced and what just flows. Notice what settles just right in your bones. Find what ignites a spark in your heart and brings light to your soul. Go that way.

Be clear about what you want. Be committed to your goals. Be consistent in your actions. Be confident in your abilities. And be courageous in your choices. Don't worry about perfection. If you can commit to this path with an open mind, willing to learn, willing to grow, willing to get a little bit better each day—you're going to go so much further than you can imagine. Good things take time. Stay patient and persistent. Show up, even when things aren't going your way. Show up imperfectly. Show up exactly as you are. Just show up. That's it. That's the secret. It's the type of magic that doesn't come from a spellbook, a potion that isn't found in a bottle. It comes from you. Your commitment, your consistency, your courage, your choices. You're the one who gets to decide how far you go.

Choose one thing that feels right to you today. Maybe it's rest. Quietness. Peace. Or maybe it's work. Hustle. Action. Whatever it is, find the thing that aligns with your inner rhythm—and say *yes* to it. Say *yes* to yourself. To your vision. To your heart's inner wisdom. Say *yes* to what supports you. To what inspires you. To the inner voice that whispers, *go this way*. Release the idea that you should be saying *yes* to everything and everyone *but you*. The world doesn't need you to be working against yourself right now. It needs you to get in alignment. And the only way to do that is by trusting yourself. Trusting that you know what you need. Trusting your own inner guidance system to lead the way. So go within. Probe deeper. What does your soul crave today? What feels good? What feels like a *yes*? If it's rest, then rest. If it's hustle, then hustle. There's no right or wrong answer as long as it feels true to *you*.

Have the courage to allow yourself to feel good for more than just fleeting moments at a time. What if *nothing bad* is coming on the horizon? What if there is no catch? What if feeling good is your purest, natural state? Instead of waiting for the next bad thing to come, look for the signs and synchronicities that light your path. Seek joy. Build your life on the foundation of inner peace. Don't give anything outside yourself the power to control your emotions. You choose your thoughts. You choose your beliefs. *You choose how you get to feel.* Step into each new day as if every moment offers a new miracle just waiting to be uncovered. Treat the path ahead like it's paved in tiny wonders. Instead of bracing yourself for disappointment and setbacks, tell yourself the story of how when one good thing happens, another will inevitably follow. You're the only one who gets to decide how life shows up for you— and how you show up for it.

The best way to take care of the future is to take care of this moment right now. And if you want to fall hopelessly in love with tomorrow, allow yourself to fall hopelessly in love with today. There's an entire path ahead of you that you can't yet see. That's okay. What can you see in this moment? What can you be in this moment? What can you do in this moment to help you take that next step forward? Your past is worth cherishing. Honoring. Learning from. Your future is worth planning for. Visualizing. Daydreaming about. But today, this moment, this next breath—this is the most important breath of all. An unrepeatable miracle. And right now, you get to decide how you're going to show up for yourself. You get to choose how you're going to show up in the world. Your power is always in this present moment. So what are you going to do? How are you going to show up? What will you create with your wholehearted presence?

The greatest gift I can give myself is permission to do things my way. In order to thrive, I need to go at my own pace, trust my own instincts, and listen to my own inner voice. *I need to stay true to what feels right to me.* The only way this dream will ever work is if I trust myself. Because if I'm always trying to follow some fabricated rules that someone else invented for what I *should* do, I'm going to burn out fast. So when it feels right to slow down, I slow down. When it feels better to speed up, I quicken my pace. I hustle and rest. I give and receive. Sometimes, I walk the same worn road others have taken before. Other times, I listen to that little nudge that points me in a different direction. And there are moments when there's friction between my head and my heart, but I know that if I meet myself in silence, the answers I need will arise. So maybe *my way* isn't the normal way. And if you ask me to explain it, I probably can't. But this is the path that feels right to me, and I'm going to trust myself.

Your *yes* feels like a soft flutter deep inside your chest. It feels like truth and alignment. It feels like the only real thing that exists. Like the only real thing that has ever existed. It feels like coming home. Your *yes* feels like looking up on a clear night and seeing the infinite cosmos open up before you. Like every star in the universe is shining just for you. Like you're viewing the world clearly for the very first time. Close your eyes. Repeat the word *yes* ten times. Notice how your heart beats softly against your chest. How your cells light up. Notice what illuminates inside you. Now, repeat the word *no* ten times. Notice the contrast. The heaviness. The density. The weight that settles over your shoulders. Next time you have to make a choice about your path ahead, ask yourself, *"What feels like a yes? What feels like a no?"* Follow the *yeses*.

These are the three words you need to activate your courage and unlock your inner power: *I'll be okay*. Because it's the truth. You're going to be okay, no matter where this path leads you. Your ability to persist isn't dependent on the things that happen outside of you—your ability to persist is based on the self-trust you've cultivated from within. So today, right now, affirm that you're going to be okay, no matter what your future holds. You're smart. You're resilient. And you've proven time and time again just how deep your inner strength flows. Once you start telling yourself that you're going to be okay, no matter the outcome—that's when life starts to open up for you. That's when the world begins to reveal its magic. That's when the path ahead will unravel in ways you never even dreamed. You just have to know that you got this. Whatever happens. However it unfolds. Trust your grit. Trust your strength of mind. Trust that no matter the outcome of your next choice, you're going to persevere.

You're going to make it. You're going to be okay. Even if you can't yet see how it's all going to come together, know that you're exactly where you need to be right now. Focus on taking the next aligned step. Trust in the unfolding of the path in front of you. Remember that you're just as worthy as anyone else to be here. They can't stop you. Only you can stop you. And you're going to do this. Keep stepping forward with the charisma that only you have—with the confidence that's uniquely yours. You're wanted. You're needed. You matter. This world is ready for you.

Does it lead you closer to yourself, or does it pull you further away? That's the question you always have to ask yourself. Does it feel like self-love or self-abandonment? Does it pour into your soul what you need? Close your eyes and see the life you envision for yourself. The life that feels *true* and *real* and *fulfilling*. The life that turns the mundane into magic—that doesn't steal your years but *gives you more*. Now—does it align with that vision? Does it bring you closer to your dreams? Because this life you envision—it's possible. I promise. It's possible. You just have to *want it* and *choose it* and know that you're not some minor, insignificant presence in this world—that you are worth more. You are meant for more. You are *chosen*. So please—follow the joy. Follow the love. Follow the pull of your beating heart. Follow what stirs your soul. Follow what shakes you from your numbness and makes you *feel*. And most of all—follow what calls to you. Because that's your path. That's your adventure. That's your way.

Trust your heart. Follow your intuition. Always try to be just a little bit braver than you were yesterday. Be strong, curious, and kind. Stay fearless in the pursuit of the thing that calls to you. And if you can't be fearless, be afraid and willing to do it anyway. Make space for moments to pause what you're doing to discover what's around you—wherever you are, however the world looks to you right now. Notice it. Pay attention. Look for the signs that have been right in front of you this entire time. Uncover something to be grateful for in every brand new day. Find the magic hidden in ordinary experiences. Step forward exactly as you are and offer your authentic self to the world. Know that nothing about you needs to be fixed. You're exactly where you're meant to be. And life? It's not going to pass you by as long as you stay present for it. So breathe. Relax. Let go. Trust in a universe where all things are possible.

I don't know what the rest of my life will look like, but I know that I don't want to spend my last breath wishing I hadn't taken for granted all the ones before. I know I don't want to look back and think, *I wish I had been braver.* And I know I don't want to always wonder about roads I could've taken if I had just believed in myself *a little bit more.* I don't know where this uncertain path is leading me, but I know that I need to find out firsthand. I need to see what can happen if I give myself a chance. I need to explore every inch of my own potential—just so I know. *Because I need to know.* I trust that what's meant for me won't pass me by, but I still need to be an active participant in this life. I can't sit around waiting for change. I have to be willing to create it myself. So I don't know what the rest of my life will look like, but what I do know is this: I'm going to spend my last breath feeling grateful that I lived it fully. And I'm going to look back and think, *Thank God for my brave heart.* And I'll never have to wonder about what could've been. Because from this breath to my last and for every sacred heartbeat in-between, I promise—I'm going to live.

And what I know is that there's something deep inside of me that keeps nudging me forward. Compelling me to go just a little bit further. Pouring dreams and ideas and possibilities in my mind for what *could be*. It tells me that I haven't yet reached the edges of my limits. That there's still a world of potential inside me that I haven't yet explored. That as well as I think I know myself, there's still so much more to uncover. And what I know is there's something deep within me that wants to find out—what else am I capable of? How brave can I be? Can I climb mountains and swim oceans and even scarier—can I be honest and open and vulnerable? Can I stay true to what feels *right* and *real* and *genuine* to this heart beating inside my chest? To the voice within that says, *this is for me*. And what I know is that I don't want to look back one day and say *I wish I would've*. I know I don't want to think about the roads I didn't travel because I was too afraid. I don't want to close myself off. I don't want to plant roots in soil that I'll soon outgrow. And maybe I know nothing. Nothing about tomorrow. Nothing about the path ahead. But still, I have to find out. Still, I have to give myself a chance. Still, I know—I have to try.

Right now, somewhere in this world, something is happening for you. A decision. A conversation. A chance encounter. People and experiences and opportunities all converging—leading straight to you. Every day, there are things happening in the background that you can't quite see. Pieces of the puzzle connecting into place. Creating a bigger picture that your short-range vision can't yet perceive. And it's going to come. The person, the thing, the opportunity, the experience that is so beyond anything you're currently imagining. And when it comes, I promise, it will be real, and it will be right, and your thinking mind may question it, but your beating heart will *know*. That this is *for you*. And right here, in this moment, something beautiful is unfolding. And you're worthy of it. You're worthy of the good things. The loving things. The unimaginably beautiful things. You're worthy of this perfect alignment. So please—keep your heart open. Trust in what's coming. Make space for that *one thing*—that one thing that's going to change *everything*.

It'll happen. On a day that starts like any other, when everything you know feels easy and predictable, something will enter your life and change *everything*. And you won't know that it's coming. You won't see the unfolding. All you'll know when it happens is *this is different* from every experience you've ever had before. And it may enter quietly. Softly. Like a gentle breeze brushing against your skin. A hint of familiarity washing over you. *Something more* that you can't quite label or define. Or it may barge straight in and turn all your neat and tidy plans—*everything you thought you knew*—upside down. And you won't be able to control it. You won't get to decide what it is or when it comes or how it unfolds. All you can do when it happens—is stay. Stay when you want to run. Stay and let the unfolding reveal itself. Stay, even when the voice in your head says *this might only be fleeting* and *it may not be real* and *this may lead to nowhere at all*. Stay. Because there will be something else that blooms within you. A voice that doesn't scream but whispers. A deep, intangible knowing. Something only you can feel that understands—*this is right*. Stay. Because all the best things are going to scare you. And all the best things are going to shake your foundation. And all the best things, still, are worth staying for.

PART 5: THIS IS FOR BREATHING
THROUGH THE HARD MOMENTS

Talent matters. Skills matter. Knowledge matters. But none of it will make a difference if you don't first believe in yourself. And not just when everything is going right. You have to believe in yourself when the odds are stacked against you. When the challenges feel insurmountable. When you're not sure where any of this is leading—or even if it's leading anywhere at all. You have to believe in yourself when you're not seeing immediate results. When you receive no external validation. When you have no tangible evidence that you're on the right path—just a feeling deep inside that you can't shake. You have to believe in yourself when nobody else does. You have to be your own greatest supporter and fiercest advocate. The person who never gives up on you has to be *you*. Because it's going to happen. You're going to make it. And one day, someone's going to ask you the secret to your success. And you're going to look straight into their eyes and tell them that you showed up for yourself every single day. You trusted your heart, even when it didn't make sense to anyone else. You chose courage over fear *over and over again*. And you believed in yourself every step of the way. That's what got you to the top of the mountain: relentless and unwavering self-belief.

You didn't come this far only to come this far. There's still so much for you to experience. So much for you to explore. So much for you to *celebrate*. You didn't pour your whole heart into this journey just to give up now. I know it can feel hard sometimes. More than hard. Frustrating. Overwhelming. Impossible. And I know there are days when you question your own choices. Should you find a safer path? Should you stop fooling yourself into believing that you can really make it? Should you turn back and cut your losses? But all I can say is that if it still feels right to you—*if it still calls to you*—then you owe it to yourself to see where this journey will lead. You can rest. You can take breaks. You can pause and breathe and realign *over and over again*. But please—please don't quit. Please don't give up on the thing that matters most. There's so much coming that your eyes can't yet see. There are pieces fitting together that your mind can't yet understand. But your heart? Your heart knows. So listen. Hear its words. Trust what you feel.

And on the really hard days, when it takes everything inside yourself just to affirm that *you're enough*, remember what it took to get here. Remember the times when you didn't want to admit it to anyone, but there was that small voice in your head that said, *Maybe this isn't worth it. Maybe I can't keep going. Maybe I'm not strong enough.* And remember that still, you found something inside yourself to make it through another day. And another. And you've made it through every impossible day you've ever lived. And can't you see? You're trying to convince yourself that *you're enough*, when actually, you're this incredible and fierce warrior. You're a powerhouse. The energy of the entire universe flows inside you. You're courageous and passionate and stunning and such a gift to everyone who has the honor of knowing you. Your kindness, your empathy, your light, your love—all of it is big and grand and extraordinary and so much more than just *enough*. So please, when you're trying to convince yourself that *you're enough*, remember who you are. Remember the path you've traveled. Remember the stubborn and resilient heart that beats inside you. Remember, still—you are so much more.

When you're hard on yourself for slipping up, remember that consistency matters more than perfection. What you do every day is more important than what you do occasionally. You can stumble. You can fall. You can even stay on the ground for an extra second and take a deep breath before you force yourself to get back up. You can make mistakes. You can be imperfect. You can be human. You can give yourself grace. You can do it wrong before you get it right. You can be extra compassionate with yourself on the days you wish you could do over. Don't let a single bad moment halt your momentum. Don't let one step back negate a hundred steps forward. Don't let yourself give up when you've come so far. Your mistakes, your slip ups, your bad days—they're all part of a beautiful journey. Take the lessons you need and carry them with you as you move forward. Keep going. Keep rising. Never forget why you started.

One day, you may realize that the mistakes you were so hard on yourself for making were never really mistakes at all. That it was never a mistake to love with your whole heart. It was never a mistake to be brave and hopeful and kind. It was never a mistake to take center stage when you've been a background character in your own life for too long. Because each of these experiences taught you something valuable. Something you needed. Something that made you stronger and wiser as a result. So don't let the mistakes of your past cause you to close your heart or stop you from taking that next step. Maybe they weren't mistakes. Maybe they were just experiences. Lessons. Growth. Maybe they were meant to serve you, not hurt you. Maybe they're just proof of a life fully lived.

Don't spend your whole life self-criticizing away your happiness. Maybe some of the things you label as wrong are only wrong in your mind. Like those weeks when you're not as productive. When you feel uninspired. When you convince yourself that you must be broken because you're not further along on your own self-imposed timeline. Maybe the solution isn't to double down and force yourself to work harder. Maybe the solution is to allow it to be—exactly as it is. To stop trying to alter the natural flow of life but to instead flow *with* life. Honor your inner rhythm. Don't let *shoulds* and *supposed tos* take up valuable space in your world. You're so hard on yourself when you don't live up to your own impossible expectations. But what if there's nothing actually wrong with where you are right now? What if everything is unfolding in perfect timing? And what if in this moment, everything is exactly as it's meant to be?

Living life without regrets doesn't mean you never hesitate, make mistakes, or second-guess your decisions every once in a while. In fact, living life without regrets requires you to do *all* these things. It means stepping forward, even when you're afraid. Choosing courage over fear. Accepting the lessons that come with defeat. It means not running from the pain that transforms you and reveals the beautiful messiness of being human. Feeling your own heart break because you had the courage to love fiercely and wholly without any guarantees that you'd receive that same love in return. It means being willing to face rejection, failure, and uncertainty without letting the fear of these experiences stop you from ever trying. It means seeking growth and transformation, even when it'd be more comfortable to stay the same. Living life without regrets doesn't mean you don't sometimes wonder what would've happened if you'd made a different choice. But you don't live in that space. You live here, in this moment, with the breath that flows through you right now. Never moving backwards. Never lessening the experiences that have shaped you. Never apologizing for a life fully lived.

It will be maddening, and some days, you will hate it. You will think about turning back all the time and question yourself nearly every step of the way. You will worry constantly that you're not doing enough, even on the days you've lost yourself in trying to do too much. You will hate the struggles when you're in them and feel grateful for them when they're over. And sometimes, you will lose yourself in the tiniest details, the smallest imperfections, and you'll have to remind yourself to step back. To breathe. To give yourself grace as you figure it out. You will have to ask yourself each morning if it's still worth it. If you still want it. And you'll have to keep choosing it, every single day. You will love it and hate it and go mad about it. But if you can stick with it—if you can reach the edges of your limits and dare to push just a little bit further—you will be in awe of how the universe opens up for you. And you'll realize you've loved the journey just as much as the destination. And the struggles, the challenges, the difficult moments when you didn't know if you could go on but somehow did—they didn't take away from your experience but instead made it fuller. Richer. Better, somehow. And all of it—all of the beautiful messiness that comes with not just existing but *living*—it will be worth it.

They don't see the late nights and early mornings. They don't see the painstaking care that you put into your work. They don't see when it's unglamorous. When it isn't pretty. They don't see the long hours when you do the exact same thing *over and over again* in order to make it *just right*. Every day, you're doing things that nobody sees. You're working in silence. Investing your time and energy into this vision you can't get out of your head. And every day, you're showing up for yourself with no guarantees that it's ever going to lead you anywhere. Nobody's watching you, crowning you with praise and adoration. Nobody's giving you awards for your commitment and consistency. There is no applause. But one day, you're going to look back on these moments, and you'll know that *this is why you made it*. You weren't lucky. It didn't just fall into your lap. You *chose* it. You sacrificed for it. You built it. And you didn't just stumble upon your success—you *succeeded on purpose*.

You will achieve all of your biggest goals and dreams, and when you look back on your journey, you'll feel so incredibly proud. But it won't be the success that you're most proud of. You'll feel proud that you followed your heart, even when people told you that you were crazy. Even when they told you it wasn't possible. Even when you started to believe they were right. You'll feel proud that you didn't let challenges deter you. That you turned obstacles into opportunities. That you kept going, even when it felt like you couldn't take another step. You'll feel proud that you did the thing you thought you couldn't do. That you took the risk. That you chose courage over fear. That you trusted your heart, even when you couldn't see the entire path ahead. The moment you achieve your goals will be absolutely brilliant. But it wouldn't be possible without your willingness to keep showing up for yourself every single day—without your courage and resilience and deep inner strength. So know that one day, you're going to look back on this moment, and it'll all make sense—why it happened this way. And you're going to be so proud of how it all unfolded. You'll be so proud of yourself for persevering. You'll be proud that through it all, you never gave up.

zanna keithley

If you only knew everything that the universe is doing to support you—how your hard work is paying off in ways you can't yet perceive. One day, you'll step back, and you'll finally see it all so clearly: how the tangled knots of your unique path unraveled in divine timing—never too early, never too late. How it all unfolded perfectly to lead you somewhere even greater than you had imagined. You'll see the magic that created your life. The beauty in the messiness. The richness of your everyday world, in all of its colors. You'll see how every long night, every early morning, every yes, every no—it was all for a reason. It all meant something. And you'll recognize how some paths had to end so others could begin. How some things had to fall apart so something new could come together. And how you had to climb your tallest mountain before you could soar. And maybe you can't see it now, but I promise, there's a reason your heart has guided you here. You're right on time. It's coming. You're exactly where you need to be.

Maybe that thing that didn't work out was actually the greatest blessing that's ever happened to you. Maybe that so-called failure was actually a gift. Maybe that rejection you received was how the universe protected you from something that would've held you back. And maybe where you are right now in this moment is exactly where you're supposed to be. Maybe you can't quite understand it yet— why it had to happen this way. But one day, you'll step back and see it all so clearly. How some experiences had to end so better ones could begin. How some things had to fall apart so greater things could come together. And how what you thought you wanted was nothing compared to what you ultimately received. So keep your heart open. Honor the journey that's brought you here today, and trust the path ahead. Nothing about your life has been a mistake. One day, you'll see—your story is unfolding beautifully.

If you don't feel it, don't force it. With people. With new experiences. With old experiences. With your artistry and creativity. And most of all—with your energy. Trust your instincts. Listen to your inner rhythm. Sometimes, you're meant to walk into the fire and pour your whole self into your excitement and passion. Other times, you're meant to lie down exactly where you are and let yourself be carried by the ocean's gentle waves. Listen to your inner voice as it guides you toward the people and experiences that are for you. Peacefully let go of what no longer feels right. Energy doesn't lie. Your innermost feelings aren't trying to sabotage you—they're meant to set you free. Trust the flow of life moving through you—working with you. Guiding you. Always showing you the way.

When you decide to live a heart-led life, you will inevitably disappoint some people. Not because you're making a mistake or doing the wrong thing. No—they'll be disappointed because you can't pretend to be who they want you to be. They'll create a vision of who they think you are in their mind, but that vision doesn't always match reality. They may want you to remain in a place that isn't right for you because it makes their life easier if you remain where you are. And they may not want you to make decisions for yourself because what you decide doesn't fit into their plans for their future. This doesn't make them bad people. But you can't base your decisions on not letting them down. Because at the end of the day, what matters most is that you don't disappoint yourself. That you don't let yourself down. So stay true to the real you, not the version of you that other people create. Follow your own sacred path. Listen to the beat of your own wild heart, and give others permission to do the same.

Does it make you feel like you need to change yourself into something you're not in order to be worthy of it? Then walk away and don't look back. Does it make you feel like you need to hide your true self in order to be accepted? Then say no and don't give it a second thought. Does it make you feel like you'll never be enough? Then unapologetically turn it down. Does it make you doubt what you're capable of achieving? Does it break you down instead of build you up? Does it take away from your confidence? Does it make you feel lesser for being exactly who you are right now? Then reject it. Deny it. Dismiss it. *Let it go.* You can peacefully say no or burn it to the ground, but whatever you do—don't go toward the thing that tries to diminish your worth. Find the sweet spot where the people and experiences you're surrounded by support your growth but also believe you're already enough. They may challenge you, but they won't belittle you. They may dare you to push yourself but only because they believe in your potential. Even if you haven't found your place in the world yet, don't settle. Don't conform. Don't be anything less than the truest, most authentic you.

You thought you were doing everything right. You're facing your fears. Making brave choices. You're even listening to your inner wisdom and trusting your heart to lead the way. *Because there has to be a reason everyone always says you should follow your heart, doesn't there?* It has to mean something. It has to work. And yet, the world keeps moving, and you're standing still. Always waiting. Never knowing if you'll actually succeed. *Maybe your intuition is broken,* you think. Maybe this whole *following your heart* thing is meant for *everyone but you.* And right now, your eyes only perceive failure and your mind only thinks *run.* But please—please don't go. Please stay. There's something happening in the universe that you can't yet quite see. But one day, you will. One day, you'll understand. And this moment right now? This moment when you have to find strength in the uncertainty and faith in the waiting. This is the moment of your transformation. And if you can just hold on a little longer, you'll see—some things are worth waiting for.

They don't tell you that facing your fears isn't even the hardest part. Yes, it's scary. But you're still in control of the narrative—you still get to choose what actions you ultimately take. We talk about fears and obstacles like they're the most difficult aspect of the journey forward. But the truth is—what they don't tell you—is that the hardest part is the waiting. Waiting for your day to come. Waiting for answers. Waiting to see if pouring your heart and energy into your daily efforts will finally pay off in a visible, tangible way. You can't control how the world responds or force it to move at your pace. All you can do is remember that there is still a life to be lived, here in the waiting. And there is peace to be found, even in the uncertainty. And when you think there is nothing more you can do as you wait for something that is beyond your control, remember that reaching those external goals won't bring you fulfillment if you can't find fulfillment in your own self right now. So this is your opportunity, here in the waiting—to go inward. To find contentment in your own being. To uncover the beauty of the life you're living right now. These long days of waiting are only a whisper of a breath in the years of your life. They won't last forever. But the solid foundation you create for yourself in these quiet moments will.

Maybe this is it. Maybe this is the one. Maybe this is the right path. The right time. The right circumstances, all coming together exactly how they were meant to. Maybe this will be woven into the fabric of every page you write from this moment. Maybe it'll be *everything*. Or maybe— maybe it'll be a single chapter. Maybe it won't turn out the way you're imagining. Maybe it isn't quite what you think. And I know that's hard because *you want it so badly*. But the best thing you can do for yourself is reframe. Instead of *it's this or nothing*, you have to tell yourself—it's going to be this or something better. It's this or something that's *truly for you*. It's this or something that's going to feel *even more aligned*. If it's not this, what's coming is going to surpass everything you're envisioning. And if this isn't for you, it's because there's something you can't quite see that's making its way toward you right now. Something that's going to far exceed everything you thought you wanted. Something real and honest and pure and true. So maybe this is it. Maybe this is the one. But if not—my goodness, just imagine what's still to come.

Step back. Slow down. Give yourself permission to pause. Take a deep breath. Rest. Recover. Realign. It's going to be okay—really. You don't need to rush through life at full speed. We spend so much time worrying that we're going to miss out on all the good stuff if we don't move fast enough, but the truth is, we have it all backwards. We miss out on all the good stuff when we're moving too fast. And I don't just mean the external experiences. The internal ones, too. The whisper of your intuition. The answer you've been seeking. The wisdom of the quiet voice within. So much goes unnoticed when you're always hurrying toward the next thing. And if you can just slow down. If you can give yourself a chance to breathe. If you can embrace the beauty of stillness. Then you'll see—so many of the things you've been chasing are going to find you.

When you're hard on yourself because you think you should be *doing* or *completing* or *achieving* more, remember this: if all you do in this life is stay true to yourself, create meaningful connections, give people a safe place to land, cultivate your unique gifts, and offer your wholehearted presence to every new experience that finds you—you're doing so much more than you'll ever realize. And if all you ever do is have one honest conversation each day. If all you ever do is show one person that they're truly seen. If all you ever do is make someone laugh. If all you ever do is remain brave and open and curious and kind. If all you ever do is honor your beating heart. If all you ever do is sit with your pain and give yourself compassion and heal and keep healing over and over again. And if all you ever do is lean deeper into grace. If all you ever do is offer love and acceptance in rooms where it feels like there is none— then, I promise, you are doing so much more than you think.

Today, I will breathe and relax. I will not try to force anything that is not meant for me. I will trust that everything is working out for my highest good. And I will create an inner world so beautiful, it spills into my outer world, and when I open my eyes, I will see magic where I didn't see it before. Today, I will follow the gentle nudges of love. And I'll take care of my soul so that it feels safe in my body. I'll stand with my feet on the ground and my hand pressed against my heart and let myself feel *everything*. Today, I will use my energy to create something beautiful from the broken pieces of the life I once knew. Today, I will trust. I will grow. I will give. And I'll keep healing, over and over again if I must. And today, through it all, I'll keep breathing. Through it all, I won't give up on myself. Because I know that no matter what, I am worth it. I am worth my time. I am worth my attention. I am worth my unconditional love.

At least once a day, close your eyes, and pay attention to your beating heart. Sink into stillness. Let the light of the universe wash over your skin. Lay down your armor, take off your disguise, and let the fortress you've built come crumbling down. Release the striving. Let go of the fighting.

Come home to yourself.

I have chosen comfort over courage, fear over faith, worry over peace, and suffering over love. But in each moment, I remember that I always have the power to choose again.

You think the heaviness you're feeling is what's wrong with you, but the heaviness is just a manifestation of something bigger happening within. Heaviness is the symptom—resistance is the disease. Resistance is what's holding you back. Resistance is what makes the air around you feel so dense. If you want to release the heaviness, you must be willing to be an observer and a participant of your own inner battles. Uncover the root of your resistance. Walk into it. Unravel it from the inside. This is the path to your transformation.

Maybe this is the good kind of heaviness. Maybe this kind of heaviness means something is shifting inside you. You're evolving. Transforming. You feel heavy because nothing about your old life feels right anymore. Don't suppress the heaviness—seek to understand. Maybe heaviness is an invitation to step into the discomfort and uncover what's changing within.

Everything in the universe is in a cycle. The seasons. The moon. Your breath. You. Nothing stays in one state forever. That's why everything feels so heavy—because you're holding onto what you were meant to release. This experience was meant to teach you. You were never meant to carry the weight of it for so long. Honor the cycle you're in by releasing what no longer serves you. Let it in, then let it go. Make space for a new season to come forth.

Shining a light into the darkest corners of your being isn't about suppressing the darkness—it's about showing your shadows they're not alone.

Release the idea that feeling grateful means never having negative thoughts or that having negative thoughts means you're not grateful enough. You can feel sad, down, and heavy while still feeling grateful for all that you have. You can love your life in all of its beautiful messiness, even on the hard days. Gratitude doesn't appear when you're happy and disappear when you're sad. It doesn't exist only in a state of perfection. Gratitude is found in all moments—the sad, the weary, the tired, the disappointed, the hurt, the mournful. You are allowed to feel sad and grateful at the same time. You are allowed to feel it all.

This year, I learned that grief and gratitude can coexist. That I can feel my heart crack down the middle and be thankful for the pain because it means that I've lived fully and loved deeply—that I didn't hide from life but instead chose to pour my whole self into the act of beautiful, hard, messy living. I learned that I can love the life I have now while still taking time to grieve the paths I didn't walk. The lives I didn't get to live. The people who are no longer traveling this path beside me. The visions of a future I once had that can no longer be. I learned that so many times in life, we don't know that the last time we do something is going to be the last. That it often sneaks up on us unexpectedly. And that while we can't prevent the lasts, we can love what we have now while it's still here just a little bit more. This year, I learned that my heart can handle so much more than I ever gave it credit for. That it's soft but mighty. That it's far stronger than I ever realized—stronger than I even know now. And while I sometimes wish it didn't have to be so strong, I'm grateful for this beating heart for always reminding me that I'm still here. Still breathing. I'm grateful for its gentle wisdom and soft nudges. And most of all, I'm grateful that in the joy and the pain, the hope and the heartache—it knows love.

I think it's beautiful how you water the earth with the love that pours out from a heart that knows indescribable joy and unimaginable grief and fall-to-your-knees pain. I think you're so much stronger and braver than you realize. You don't see it because you don't think you have a choice. You wear resilience across your chest like it's woven into the fabric of your skin. You carry wounds that have pierced through your bones and melded into your core. A part of you now. A part of you always. You could've chosen to harden and close yourself off from the heaviness that comes with being a tenderhearted human with nowhere to put all this love that gets left behind. But somehow, these experiences that could've broken you have made you softer. Every day, you step out from the four walls you could've hidden behind and take all the love that's still left inside you, and you pour it out. And I know this road hasn't been easy, and you don't always know the next step. But I think the fact that your heart is still open and you're still trying says more than you'll ever know. Maybe you don't always see it, but your love is a force. Your light is a constellation, illuminating the night sky—steady and enduring and brighter than you can possibly realize.

I know you're feeling a little lost and uncertain. Something is shifting inside you, and it's hard and uncomfortable, and you wish it was over. You want to be on the other side— healed and whole and immersed in a new chapter. No longer battling these demons in your mind. And I know you want to rush through this experience and get past all the discomfort. You just want to feel like *you* again. But I promise, one day, you're going to look back on this moment, and you're not going to think of these days as wasted time. This won't be the lost era or when your life fell apart. No—you're going to remember that this was when it all came together. *This was when you found yourself.* Here, in your own darkness. Here, in this space where it sometimes feels like the walls are closing in on you. Here, you unearthed something that changed *everything*. And you'll recognize what a beautiful thing it is—how you're gently feeling into each moment. How you're practicing grace. How you're slowly letting go of the weight of what's no longer for you. The discomfort you're experiencing won't last forever. But what emerges from the unraveling will. And one day, you'll understand—how this was the season of your becoming. Blooming beautifully. Transforming tenderly. Here, even as you keep doing your best just to navigate your next breath. Here, in the uncertainty. One day, you'll see—this was how you found your way.

You've come so far. Take a deep breath. Give yourself grace. You don't always have to look for another mountain to climb. You don't always have to be in the pursuit of your next-level self. Step back. Pause. *Breathe.* Can you see it? How your current-level self is already so completely worthy. Worthy of love. Worthy of compassion. Worthy of being seen, being known, being felt. And do you remember? Do you remember what it took to get here? Do you remember the fears you've overcome? The false stories and limiting beliefs you've worked so hard to release? Do you remember how scary it was to break out of your comfort zone? How so many times, you thought about turning back—but you didn't. *You didn't.* You didn't settle. You didn't quit. And God knows, it would've been so easy. So take a moment—let your soul breathe. Honor the road you've traveled to get here. Acknowledge the struggles you've faced, the bravery you've shown, the resilience of your beating heart. None of this has been easy, but here you are. Celebrate how beautifully you've bloomed.

There's peace in trusting that you are exactly where you're meant to be right now. There's peace in slowing down. In taking time to pause. In reminding your anxious mind that what's meant for you isn't going to pass you by. There's peace in knowing that no feelings are bad feelings. No seasons are bad seasons. Sometimes, you just have to let yourself feel your way through the heaviness of being human in a life that rarely feels easy and in a world that doesn't always make sense. There's peace in recognizing that the moon is allowed to honor all of its phases—and so are you. So when you don't feel at peace, remember that it's okay to contract, go inward, and seek solace in your own inner world. It's okay to stay there for a while. It's okay to just be. There's peace in knowing—no matter what phase you're in, you are still right where you need to be. Your light is still more than enough. You are still whole.

Positive thinking isn't seeing the world through rose-colored glasses. It doesn't mean that you ignore any heaviness you're feeling or that you cover up your pain with false optimism. Positive thinking is steady strength. It's the ability to keep an open mind when things don't happen the way you had hoped. You may feel the sting of disappointment, but you're also willing to see how it plays out—to trust that sometimes, things don't happen the way you wanted because something *better* is unfolding. Positive thinking is believing in the inherent goodness of the world. It's knowing that when you can't find the good outside of you, you can still *be* the good. You can still *be* the love. You can still *be the light* the world so desperately needs. Positive thinking is the quiet breath you take when you know you've done the best you can do today. That you'll try again tomorrow. That you'll never stop believing in life's magic. It's finding gratitude in the little moments. Uncovering miracles in your everyday world. Keeping your feet on the ground, rooted in this moment. Releasing control. Allowing life to work through you. It's faith. Trust. Resilience. It's a quiet strength. A gentle power. A belief in something *more*.

When I tell you to follow your heart, I'm not telling you it's going to be easy. I'm not saying that you won't sometimes hate it—that you won't think about turning back nearly every day. When I tell you to follow your heart, I'm not saying you're going to love every outcome, or that the things that happen today will make sense to you right now. I'm not telling you that there won't be detours and dead ends. That you won't get tired. That you won't sometimes wonder if this was all a mistake. Too often, we think following our heart means that the path is going to be paved in the golden light of clarity and peace. But this is rarely true. The path that your heart guides you on can be bumpy and fragmented. Each new step may always carry a lingering aura of uncertainty. It may require deep breaths and more trust than what's comfortable. But in the end, it will be worth it. Because it will be beautiful, and it will be real, and it will be the greatest gift you can ever give yourself. It will be harder than you can imagine but better than you ever dreamed. And it will be yours. Your life. Your story. Your journey. *Yours*. So when I tell you to follow your heart, I'm not telling you it's going to be easy. But what I'm saying is—you owe it to yourself to see where it might lead.

When they ask you how you made it, you're going to tell them it didn't come easy. You weren't lucky. You didn't get handed anything. And the path you walked upon wasn't perfectly paved with lights and signs that showed you the way. When they ask you how you made it, you're going to tell them you nearly lost yourself a thousand times. That you crawled over the gnarled roots of your insecurities and swam through the muddy waters of your fears. You walked through dark forests alone for endless nights with the only guiding light coming from the north star beating inside your chest. And you gave your blood and tears for it. You fell to your knees for it. You risked it all for something that came with no promises or guarantees. But still, when they ask you how you made it, you're going to tell them there was no other choice. That your heart beats for it. That your lungs breathe for it. And that the long path that led you here is the best thing you've ever done. And from the hardship, you found peace. From the darkness, you found your light. And in the end, you made it because the unfailing heart inside your chest didn't know how to quit.

And you are going to have beautiful days and devastating days and light days and heavy days, and there will be chapters when the *heavy* and *devastating* feel like they're all you've ever known. And you're going to break down and break open and feel like the pain has buried itself in your lungs and in your cells and in your soul until you don't know *you from it* or *it from you*, like it's melded into your bones and intertwined with the intangible part of you that nobody else can see. And you will run and run and want to keep running until *your shadows can no longer chase you* and *you can no longer breathe* and *this pain doesn't feel so unbearable*. And you will keep sitting with the pain and sitting with the pain *and sitting with the pain*, and some days, it'll feel a little lighter, and other days, it'll feel like the entire ocean is crushing your chest and everything is heavy and *is this the way it'll always be?* But in time, slowly, the weight will lift and the wounds will start to heal and that first unencumbered breath will be the best thing you've ever known. And you'll begin to let go of this burden you've been carrying and remember what it's like to be *you* again, and you'll uncover that inner spark within you that's been there all along. And you'll turn your pain into your purpose and use it to try to help other people feel *a little lighter* and *a little less alone* and *a little more seen*. And the pages will keep turning and a new chapter will begin, and this time, you're going to walk forward *a little less afraid*. And you're going to live every inch of this beautiful and messy and wondrous human experience. Because this—this is what you're here for.

And the really amazing thing—the thing you need to remember—is that there's still so much waiting for you up ahead. And some of your best days? They're still coming. And you haven't yet met everything that's meant for you. You haven't yet encountered all the joy and love and fulfillment that's on its way. I know it's hard to see it now, but you're going to meet people who will enter your life and feel like they've been there all along. You're going to experience miracles and synchronicities that make it feel like there really is something *more* out there in this world. Like maybe you're not alone. Like maybe this universe really is on your side. Working in your favor in ways that you can't always see. And you're going to feel it all. Rushes of exhilaration. Heart-pounding elation. Peaceful silence. Love that feels too big and great to be boxed in or contained. *Like something this beautiful shouldn't actually exist.* There's so much coming. And you still have so much time. It's not going to miss you. You just have to be present. To be here. To see it when you're in it and not when it's long passed you by. You just have to be brave and open and honest and willing. You just have to let it in.

PART 6: THIS IS FOR HONORING YOUR HEART-LED PATH

At first, you waited. You waited for someone to show up, take you by the hand, and lead the way. You waited for someone to come along and see your potential. To look at you and just know—*you're something special.* You waited for someone to choose you. But when that didn't happen, you clenched your fists, took a deep breath, and finally, you chose yourself. You made your own way. And maybe it was imperfect. Maybe you made a thousand mistakes. Maybe some days, the only things that carried you through were deep breaths and the tiniest spark of hope that just wouldn't fade. Because you knew, *if you only want something when it's easy, you don't really want that thing at all.* But you still wanted it, even when it wasn't easy. Even when you had to fight for it. Even on your hardest days. So you carved your own path. You made it happen. And looking back on your journey, you can see it so clearly now—how everything changed the day you stopped looking outside yourself and realized it was you who you needed all along.

It starts with a dream: a vision of a life that excites you. That lights you up. That brings you to your knees. You write down this vision and turn it into a goal, and you decide what you need to do to achieve this goal. From this goal, you create a plan. Your plan isn't complete, though. There are holes where you're not sure how you'll get from A to B. You might call these holes *uncertainties* at first, but in time, you discover they're actually *possibilities*. They help you to remain open to the unexpected. To find opportunities where you didn't see them before. You follow this plan, one small step at a time, trusting your intuition to guide you forward. And it may happen in a single grand moment, or it may sneak up on you unexpectedly, but one day, you'll look around in awe as you discover the vision you once had is now your reality. You created this. You made the abstract real and the impossible *possible*. And you never needed any special powers or abilities to get here. It all happened because you had a dream in your heart and the courage to take the first step.

Maybe everything that has happened this past year has been leading you to your true destiny. Maybe this is the beginning of a new chapter. The *something more* you've felt deep within for so long is finally showing up in your outer world. The seeds you've planted are now beginning to grow into something more beautiful than you ever could've imagined. The internal work you've been doing is being reflected outside of you. I know it's been a long journey, but it couldn't happen overnight. The unraveling has been hard and heavy, but it was needed. Because now, you're ready. Now it's time to let it in. The love. The abundance. The fulfillment. The *something more* is here. And it's going to be even better than you thought. This next chapter is going to take your breath away. The entire universe is working together to delight you with its magic.

I think the next plot twist is that things are about to get really good. I think this world is going to open up for you in unimaginable ways. I think you're walking into your best chapter yet. And finally, you're going to see where all of this has been leading. Your hard work hasn't been for nothing. How you keep showing up. How you keep picking yourself back up. How you never give up on this dream, this vision, this feeling deep within that says *this is for you*. How you never give up on yourself. All along, it was paying off in ways you couldn't see. And even when you couldn't find proof in the outside world that anything was working out, you listened to your heart's wisdom and continually leaned into faith and trust. But now—now you're going to see it. The proof. The illumination of something more beautiful than you can even imagine. You're going to see where the universe has been guiding you. And it's going to be better than you can possibly know.

The goal is not to one day look back on your life and say, *this is the life I was given*. The goal is to one day look back on your life and say, *this is the life I chose*. I *chose* my opportunities. I *chose* the experiences that shaped me. I chose to *pick myself back up* when I stumbled to the ground. I chose to create my own path. To set forward on my own grand adventure. I chose to believe in myself—to trust where my heart was leading me, even when it didn't make sense to anyone else. I chose my thoughts, my beliefs, and my actions—my perceptions of the world have been entirely up to me. And I chose to be hopelessly infatuated with being alive. To not settle for anything less than perfect love. Perfect peace. Perfect exhilaration for each and every breath that has flowed through my lungs. This life may be messy and imperfect and sometimes chaotic, but it's my messiness. My sweet imperfections. My beautiful chaos. I chose it once, and I'd choose it again. Today. Tomorrow. Always.

When I say *I hope you live an extraordinary life*, I'm not saying, fill it with gold medals and external achievements. I don't mean, make it shiny and impressive. And I'm not saying that you need to *do* more or *be* more or *have* more—that you should always strive for *more*. No—when I say *I hope you live an extraordinary life*, what I mean is, I hope you create something that feels good from the inside, even if it doesn't look glamorous from the outside. I hope you spend an exorbitant amount of time watching the sky and breathing fresh air. I hope you make space for the quiet moments—that you prioritize your own inner peace. I hope you live your days with an open heart. I hope you never abandon yourself—that you always travel this road with the companionship of your own genuine, unconditional love. I hope you connect with yourself, with others, and with the world around you in a deeply meaningful and profound way. I hope you know great love and great joy and great fulfillment. And more than anything, I hope you know how to find these things within yourself first. When I say *I hope you live an extraordinary life*, what I really mean is, I hope you make your own rules. I hope you do it your own way. I hope that through it all, you stay true to you.

Your soul's version of dancing in the rain is to release your worries and choose to love this moment right now, exactly as it is. To create your happiness instead of waiting for it. To uncover quiet miracles and tiny wonders in every ordinary aspect of your daily life. To live with your heart wide open. To be courageous in the face of the unknown. To let go of how you think life *should be* and allow everything to be *what it is*. To let people be who they are. To let experiences unfold just as they're meant to. And most of all, to allow yourself to be all that you are and all that you were meant to be without denying a single part of what makes you gloriously and unapologetically you. Your soul's version of dancing in the rain is to love the journey just as much as the destination. To be here right now, in this moment. With your eyes wide open. Your feet steady on the ground. Ready to live not just the length of your life but the breadth of it, too.

The path to success isn't paved solely in personal development and self-improvement. It's not always about the books you read, the podcasts you listen to, or the courses you take. The path to success is also paved in the pauses. The energy you put into doing should be balanced with the energy you put into being. Step back. Read a book for fun. Watch the show that always makes you laugh. Meet your best friend for coffee. Dance to your favorite music. Let the sunshine wash over your skin. Uncover the beauty that exists in your life right now. Balance effort with ease. Let the slowdown be just as important as the hustle. Find the things that capture your heart's imagination, then follow your curiosity just to see where it takes you. Take care of the future by taking care of this moment right now. Nourish your spirit. Feed your soul. Breathe. Surrender. Let go.

Every once in a while, pause in the pursuit of doing all the things your future self will thank you for and simply be your future self. Take a step back and acknowledge how far you've come. Thank yourself for everything you've done that's led you to where you are today. Put your own name at the top of your gratitude list. Feel sincerely proud of yourself. Even if you aren't exactly where you want to be, you've come so far. You've committed so much of yourself. You've made leaps you never thought you could make. You've chosen courage over fear and self-trust over self-doubt. Can't you see how extraordinary it is to choose this path? This isn't easy, and you're doing it. *You're doing it.* So pause. Step back. Take a look at what you've accomplished so far. Acknowledge the courage and strength it's taken to get here. You're not simply existing. You're creating. You're thriving. You're *living*.

So often, we say that we wish we had known back then what we know now. We dream of returning to our pasts so we can make new choices. So we can live more fully. So we can cherish what we had while we had it and love it all just *a little bit more*. But we can't go back. And if we're always dreaming of going back, we're going to miss out on what we have right now. And one day, *today* is the day we'll be wishing we could return to—today is the day we'll wish we had loved just *a little bit more*. So this is what we can do: we can give this present moment our undivided attention. We can tell the people we love exactly how we feel while they're here. We can take the risks we've been so afraid to take and choose bravery over backing down. And every once in a while, we can step out of our thinking minds and into our feeling hearts. We can be here, exactly where we are, without always searching for something to change or fix. And we can give this whole living thing our very best shot. Maybe we can't go back and change the past, but we can create a present moment so beautiful that it doesn't need to be changed.

I don't want to miss the magic of this day. I don't want to spend the next twelve hours living inside my head. I don't want to always stay hidden behind closed doors when right outside these four walls, the sun is waking up, painting the sky with colors that don't exist inside my cell phone. I don't want to not open my eyes. To not pause and breathe. To not notice the world moving around me. I don't want to blink and find that this day is already just a fleeting memory. I don't want to spend my entire life lamenting that time goes by too fast and always dwelling on the past like the present doesn't exist. I don't want to make excuses for why I haven't called old friends. For why I no longer remember the scent of ocean air and wildflowers. For why I haven't looked up at the stars in so long. I don't want to miss the magic of this day. Of this life. I don't want to get to the end of this chapter and realize I was never really here at all. So at least for today, I'm going to try to be here now, as best as I can. And I'm going to feel my heart beating inside my chest. I'm going to open my eyes and watch the sky and give myself permission to just breathe. And at least for today, I'm going to be present for these sacred moments while I have them. And that—that will be enough.

I am learning how to balance watching my life through a phone screen and experiencing it through all of my senses. I am figuring out how to live in the moment while capturing images I can carry with me forever. I am discovering how to honor my past while living fully in this present moment. I am learning how to love with my whole heart while not clinging onto anything that's no longer meant for me. I am discovering how I can embrace my light while not neglecting my shadows. I am learning how to make space for my transformation while loving every version of me I've ever been. I am figuring this out, one day, one minute, one second at a time. I expand and I contract, and I breathe in the space between, and I transcend.

Have I looked in the mirror today? Have I paused and gazed into my own eyes? Have I pressed my palm against my chest and felt the soft beating of my stubborn heart? Have I glanced up at the sky? Have I listened to the sounds of the world in motion? Have I remembered why I'm here? Not just to exist but to live. And did I live? Was I here? *Really here.* Not just going through the motions but *present.* Vibrant. Alive. Was I brave and curious and kind? Did I make this present moment as beautiful as I could while planting seeds for my uncharted future? I think about getting to the end and answering no to all these questions, and I think—*no.* No, that won't do. I'm here right now, and there are colors that exist in this world that I still haven't seen. There are breadcrumbs to follow. Discoveries to unearth. There's a spark inside of me that I still haven't stirred. So today, I plant my feet on the ground and watch the sky and honor the wisdom of my beating heart. And I breathe. I let go. I live.

When I look back on my life, I will love the first timid steps as much as the big successes. I will be as proud of the small moments of courage as I am of the giant moments of achievement. I will know there were no wasted days. Everything had a purpose. Everything had meaning. The small actions of my daily life were as profound as the big ones. And there was always beauty to be found in every quiet and unassuming moment. But I won't wait until the end of my life to find the good, and I won't wait until it's all over to love the moment I'm in right now. When I look back on my life, I will love the big and small and the in-between, but most of all, I will love that I lived every part of it. From the outside in and the inside out—I lived.

If you woke up today with the opportunity to add another page to the story of your life, then you owe it to yourself to create the most beautiful story you can imagine. Whatever that is. However that looks to you. Let the ink spill onto the blank page and fill the empty lines with the magic you thought was *out there* but was really inside you this whole time. Write a story of hope and redemption. Of strength and perseverance. Of falling apart and having the courage to pick up the broken pieces and put yourself back together again. Write about how you intimately know grief and heartbreak because you had the courage to love with your whole heart, even when you had no guarantees that you'd receive the same love in return. Let the ink smear across the page from all the moments you laughed so hard that your tears left a permanent mark on the unwritten pages of your future. And let the spaces between words be quiet pauses of appreciation. Deep breaths and spiritual resets. Gratitude for a life fully lived. If you woke up today with the opportunity to add another page to the story of your life, then you owe it to yourself to write the story of how you lived it fully. Messy and afraid but hopeful and brave. Heart open. Vision clear. Always looking towards the sun.

And one day, there will be a last. A last sunrise. A last morning coffee. A last late night conversation. A last glance up at the moon. Maybe I'll know that day when it greets me. Maybe I'll open my eyes and recognize that today isn't like the rest. Or maybe it will feel just like yesterday—just like all the ones before. Maybe I won't get to choose what I do or say because *I didn't know*. I didn't know that this was all going to end and I still didn't . . . *I still didn't do what?* That's the question, isn't it? What are the missing puzzle pieces? The dreams in my heart that I haven't yet followed. The fears I told myself I would one day face. What's out there in this vast universe that I still haven't explored? And what about the world within me? What's still left undiscovered in there? And did I offer love with an open heart? Did I allow myself to receive it? Did I get to meet enough people and exchange stories and learn their secret smile and what makes their heart skip a beat? And did I pause? Did I remember to look up? Did I watch the sky today? Those are the questions—the breadcrumbs that I follow until the last. The last sunrise. The last morning coffee. The last late night conversation. The last glance up at the moon.

At first, life was something that happened to you. When something undesired happened in your outer world, you thought you were being punished. And when you tried talking to the universe, you'd receive no clear response. So you started to believe that you'd been abandoned. Forgotten. Unseen. Slowly, though, you began to realize that maybe these bad moments weren't so bad at all. With each challenge you faced, you learned you could tap into an endless reservoir of inner strength and resilience that gave you more confidence as you moved forward. And sometimes, these hardships led you to something that was even better than what you had originally hoped for. And you realized, maybe life wasn't something that happened to you. Maybe it was all happening for you. And in time, your trust deepened. With each challenge, your faith was only reinforced. And then, one day, something changed—not in one single moment but in a series of tiny little wonders. Life wasn't just happening to or even for you anymore—it was happening through you. And you realized your purpose was so much greater than you had ever believed. And maybe, just maybe, you were created exactly as you are because who you are is who this world needs.

And in the end, I hope you can say, *I never made a mistake that I didn't learn from. I never met a challenge that didn't make me stronger. I never walked a path that didn't hold some kind of treasure*—*even the broken trails that led to brick walls and dead ends. They still meant something. They still mattered.* And I hope you can say, *Thank God for the path that led me here today. This imperfect, messy, beautiful journey. These scars of mine tell stories of unimaginable strength. These eyes of mine tell stories of deep and expansive love.* I hope your memories aren't wrapped in regrets and what ifs but in deep appreciation for the courageous heart beating inside your chest. I hope you can say that you poured love into the world and the world poured love back into you. I hope one day you look back and see a path filled with tiny wonders—with inexplicable miracles and beautiful synchronicities. Proof that the universe was always on your side, working in ways you didn't always understand. And in the end, I hope you can say, *This journey didn't harden me. No*—*I grew softer. This journey didn't close my heart. No*—*I opened it wider. This journey didn't lessen my belief in magic. No*—*I've seen it firsthand.*

A success story: you pour countless hours into your craft only to find yourself continually moving backwards. You make mistakes. So many mistakes. You do it wrong over and over again. You try a different approach, and it doesn't work out. New challenges appear almost daily. You begin to wonder if all these roadblocks are the universe's way of telling you this isn't for you. As soon as you think it, though, you know that isn't true. And at the end of each day, you ask yourself, *"Do I really want to do this again tomorrow?"* The answer that comes is always the same: *Yes.* So you keep showing up. You keep pouring your heart into this thing you love. It's a part of you. In your bones and in your body and in the blood that runs through your veins. And there's a vision of what this could be that only you can see. You replay this vision in your head over and over again. You persist, even when no one else can see what you can. And slowly, things begin to shift into place. Small wins, followed by bigger ones. The world opening up for you. Working in your favor. It's not luck. It's you. It's your courage and resilience. It's your tenacity. Your patience. Your grit. You wrote this story with the strength of your beating heart. And the day you realize nobody can take that away from you—that's the success.

Thank you for sharing your gift. I know how hard it can be to offer something to the world that feels sacred to you. Your voice. Your art. The creation that started as only a glimmer of an idea in your mind—an idea that you molded and built and nurtured so carefully. That you brought to life. It can be tempting to want to hold your gift close so it can't be polluted with other people's criticisms. To lock it up somewhere safe. To keep it under wraps. But possession isn't the same thing as love. And if you really love something, you have to set it free. Because if you give it a chance to soar, it's going to find so many worthy homes throughout this world in the hearts of people who need the exact thing you can give. Offering your divine gift is an expression of love. So thank you for sharing it. Thank you for the art and humor and wisdom you offer that connects us. That unites us. That heals our hearts and replenishes our souls.

this is how you find your way

And now I can see. How when I stopped fighting my own intuition and let it guide my next steps, it always led me to exactly where I needed to be. To people and places, to experiences and opportunities—all that taught me, that strengthened me, that gave me exactly what I didn't know I needed at the time. *And now I can see.* How when I finally did the thing my mind so badly didn't want to do—*the thing the universe had been gently nudging me toward all along*—it was never as terrible as my imagination had made it out to be. How, in fact, every time I did that hard and scary thing, it usually ended up becoming one of the greatest things I've ever done. *And now I can see.* How when I clung so tightly to what wasn't for me, I was blocking what *was* for me from coming forward. And when I finally let go, that's when something truly beautiful would emerge. All along, it was just waiting for me to let it in. *And now I can see.* How when I stopped trying to control the narrative, the story that unfolded was far greater than anything I could've written. Far richer. Far more fulfilling. Far better than the pristine, challenge-free plotline I would've created if I held the pen. *And now I can see.* Now I know. Now I understand. That this beating heart won't steer me wrong. That I can trust the universe. That I can trust what I feel. And I can trust that the unknown path ahead will always lead me exactly where I need to go.

Oh this heart of mine. So stubborn. So soft. As gentle as a summer breeze. As fierce as the ocean waves. This heart inside me feels *everything*. It knows euphoric joy and profound grief. It feels sweeping love and shattering pain. And when my mind wants to run and hide from the hard parts of living, my heart whispers—*no, stay*. So I stay. And I breathe. And I keep my feet on the ground, and *I feel it all*. Because my heart knows that the only way out is through. And the only way to truly live is to *feel*. And this heart—it finds so much to live for. It loves good food and genuine connection. It beats for late night conversations about where we come from and the infinite nature of our souls. It loves to see and be seen. To feel and be felt. To listen and to speak. This heart of mine dreams. It wishes. And oh, how it *believes*. It believes in magic and possibilities—in what my eyes can't see and my mind can't perceive. It nudges me forward when I'm afraid. It tells me to trust. To lean in. To let go. This heart of mine has endured so much. So much sorrow, so much pain. But still, it grows softer. Still, it opens wider. Still, it loves deeper. And I know that when I'm looking for guidance, for answers, for a sign—I can start right where I am. Here, in my heart. That's where I find freedom. That's where I find understanding. That's where I find myself.

This is what they can't take from you: they can't take the morning sunrise. The promise of a new moon. The feel of the earth against your bare feet. They can't take your history—the hope and the heartache. The experiences that shaped you. How you felt your heart crack down the middle and sewed it back together with your own two hands. They can't take your deep inner strength or the resilience you've built after years of enduring, persisting, *surviving*. They can't take your stubborn heart and how it beats through the joy and the pain. Steady. Constant. Refusing to quit. They'll never take your love for stories and how a really good one can plant itself in your heart and stay with you long after you've reached the end. They can't take the wisdom that lives inside you. Your heart's consciousness. That feeling deep within that can't be put into words. They can't take your hope for the future. Your vision of tomorrow. Your belief in something more. They can't take your enormous heart and endless capacity to love. They can't take your soul. Your essence. The part of you that's infinite, measureless, and everlasting. They can't take your roots that keep you anchored to the ground. And no matter how hard the wind blows, you remain firm in your sense of being. Steady. Strong. Unshaken.

These days, it's no longer about achieving gold medals and getting recognition, as if that's some kind of proof that I have value in this world. I don't chase the feeling of being liked by everyone I meet. And I'm no longer consumed with chiseling at the core of who I am in an attempt to make myself fit into spaces I was never meant for, no matter how hard I tried. No—these days, I'm falling in love with waking up before sunrise and watching the stars as they catch their last breath before the night sky transforms into a symphony of pale pinks and soft yellows and baby blues. I'm falling in love with sinking into stillness. Letting silence wrap around me. Closing my eyes and following the threads back to my beating heart. I'm falling in love with city streets and crowded spaces—with the hum of life vibrating through the air and settling deep into my bones. I'm falling in love with sharing spaces with people who give me a safe place to display my quirks and weirdness and everything that I've hidden in the past. With people who make me feel like I'm meant to be here—like their hearts were always meant to match mine. And I'm falling in love with unknown tomorrows. With a future where I can't see what's coming. With releasing control and letting life do its thing without always needing to take the reins. And these days, I'm falling in love with my own gentle spirit. With the way laughter sounds upon my own lips. With my soft, stubborn heart. With all of me. With everything I am.

And these days, I allow myself to get lost on purpose because I know that I'll always find my way. I still don't always have the right answers, but I trust my ability to figure it out. And if I get it wrong sometimes, I may feel frustrated at first. But then I breathe. And I give myself grace. And I try again. And I'll keep trying and trying as many times as I need to. Because I may give up on unaligned paths and what my heart knows isn't for me, but I'll never give up on myself. And I'm still not yet where I want to be, but I'm able to step back and recognize how far I've come. And I have bad days. Hard days. Heavy days. I get frustrated and angry. I feel sad and hurt. And I start to question the purpose of it all and wonder if my life really is just random—maybe none of this ever had any meaning at all. But I no longer stay in that place for very long. Because all I have to do is step outside and watch the sky and I can feel it—there's something more that I can't quite see. And these days, I don't hide from the thing that scares me like I used to. I may hesitate, but in the end, I'll walk toward my own discomfort if it means creating the most honest and beautiful life I can imagine for myself. And slowly, step by step, breath by breath, I navigate this path. And I trust what I can't see but what I can feel. I honor my own magic. And I stay true to my beating heart.

And one day, you realize, after all this time—the path has been inside you all along. That for so many years, you've been seeking external solutions. Quick fixes that you hoped could somehow permanently quell this war that's been waging in your mind. The war with yourself—with this enormous and overwhelming desire to be *accepted* and *wanted* and *loved*. And the answer has always been to try to control how people see you. To make sure they only get the version of yourself that you choose. The version of you that *you think they want*. And you believe you have to *do* more and *be* more and *achieve* more. And maybe one day, it'll be enough. But it's never enough. There's always *one more thing*. And there will always be *one more thing* if you keep staying on this path. Because those external solutions? They're not the way. They won't give you what you seek. No—what you're searching for is in the place you've been avoiding. You have to lie on the ground and place your hand on your heart and do nothing but listen to it beat. You have to visualize every version of yourself you've ever been and show them the love and compassion they never received. You have to open up wide and give people a chance to see and know every part of you—even the parts you've been trying to hide for so long. The path is inside you. And taking it is going to be the hardest thing you've ever done. But everything you've been searching for is right there. And if you want to know true acceptance and love and freedom—that's where it begins.

Sometimes, I think—*I hope it works out. I hope it's for me. I hope this happens and that happens. I hope the path leads to where I want it to go.* And I feel myself getting attached to certain outcomes. Things I have no control over. So I pause and take a deep breath and remember—I can't control it all. I can't control what happens tomorrow. I can't control what people do or how they feel. I can't control where this path leads me. And that can feel scary at times, but then I also remember—none of that really matters. *It doesn't matter.* Because this is what I can do: I can stay aligned with my authentic self. I can follow my joy and give it away. I can be brave when I'm called to and pour my whole mind and body and soul into every new experience that finds me. I can keep connecting with my innermost self. I can allow life to flow through me. *And I don't need to control what's out there.* I just need to stay true to what feels right. I just need to keep cultivating my own inner peace. I just need to trust my heart's deepest wisdom. *That's what I can do.* That's my power. That's my magic.

You leave behind tiny, beautiful breadcrumbs in all the places you visit and in all the lives you touch. Pieces of your energy still remain in the rooms you've walked through and in the spaces you've traveled and on the soil where you've stood. Your presence still lingers in the minds of people you once knew. Words you once said are still playing on a loop in someone's head. In someone's heart. Deeply ingrained within their very being. But it's more than just your words that stay with them. It's your energy. It's the way you've made people feel—that's what persists long after everything else fades. It's the laughter that echoes and the warmth that radiates from the inside out. And I know you don't always see it. I know you don't think it's anything special—that for you, it comes naturally to share your light. To make everything a little more beautiful than you found it. But I hope that one day, you can see it all so clearly. I hope you know how much you matter. I hope you realize that you've made such a difference. I hope you feel in your heart the undeniable truth that this world is a better place because you exist.

Continue. Continue to make choices that feel right to you, even when it means trusting your heart's wisdom over the outside voices that may sound smart and practical and logical, but still—*they're not you.* They don't hear the inner whispers. They don't feel the soft nudges. They don't know the sacred language your heart speaks. Continue to pursue your curiosities and passions and the things that make you feel most alive. Continue to reach for the people who make you feel *seen* and *safe* and *known*—the people whose presence wraps around you like a warm blanket and offers a safe place to land. Continue to slowly and gently peel off the bandages and nurture the wounds that you've been covering for so long—these scars you've been hiding that only ever wanted to be seen. Continue to contract on the days when you need to close the blinds and sit in silence and listen to the soft hum of your own breathing. A gentle reminder that you're still here. Still alive. Still whole. Continue to illuminate dark spaces with the light of your kindness and compassion. Continue to be a vessel of joy and humor and laughter. Continue to set your own rules for how your life is supposed to feel and look. Continue to be you, exactly as you are. Continue to radiate your unique and irrepressible light. Just please—continue.

"Thank you for sharing your magic." It's the strangest and most beautiful compliment. Because you hear it and think, me? Magic? I'm not doing anything special. I'm just being me. I'm just following what feels right. I'm just doing what I know. *But that's exactly it.* It's those things you don't think twice about. Those things that feel as natural as breathing. It's when you make people feel seen. When you make them feel valued. When you offer kindness in the face of unkindness. When you give without expecting anything in return. It's when you continually lean into love and goodness in a world that doesn't always feel so loving and good. You don't think of it as magic because it's just who you are. It's woven into the fabric of your being. For you, there is no other choice. But that's where it's hidden—in the small things you label as ordinary that other people see as extraordinary. That's your magic.

The real magic is when you don't know how it's going to happen. You don't know if you're ever going to make it. You don't know where this road will take you—or if it's even taking you anywhere at all. But still, you step forward and keep showing up, even on your hardest days. Sometimes, your steps are small. Other times, they're a little bigger. But you're not worried about the pace because you trust that *what's meant for you won't miss you*—that you're exactly where you're meant to be in this moment. The real magic is when your mind tries to convince you that *you can't*, but you step forward and try anyway because your beating heart tells you that *you can*. The real magic is *you*. It's your courage and commitment. Your belief in a universe where all things are possible. Your refusal to listen to the outer voices over that quiet voice within. It's in your breath. It's in your energy. *It's who you are at your core.* You're the gift. You're the spark. You're the magic.

ACKNOWLEDGEMENTS

To Mom, Dad, Melissa, Matthew, and Eric—Thank you for always supporting me, believing in me, and rooting for me. Thank you for loving me. Thank you for this really beautiful life you've given me. This book is for you.

To Angel, Logan, Jeremiah, Matilda, Rocket, and Zeke—I hope you always stay true to yourself. I hope if someone tries to tell you that you can't do something, you show them that you can. I hope you always trust the pull of your wild, beating heart. I hope you follow your dreams and explore the limitless depths of your potential. I hope you know that nothing is impossible. I hope you never forget what a gift you are.

To my Instagram supporters—I am in awe of you every single day. I hope you know how incredibly grateful I am for how you continually uplift me. It honestly takes my breath away. You pour so much love into me, and I'll always do my best to pour the love you give me back out into the world. From the bottom of my heart—thank you.

And to family and friends who have supported me on this journey—I can never adequately express what your support has meant to me. None of this would exist without you. Thank you for making me feel seen, known, valued, and loved. Thank you for being a source of love and strength in my lowest moments. Thank you for celebrating my wins, sometimes even before I realize they've happened. (Looking at you, Kristen and Sam.) I am forever grateful.

Zanna Keithley is an author, poet, and social media content creator living in Seattle, Washington. She's been writing since she was a kid, when she would spend hours filling notebooks with her own deleted scenes to *Spice World*. She's a devoted St. Louis Cardinals fan and a lifelong sports lover who, at any given moment, is likely playing in multiple fantasy sports leagues with her family.

You can find her on Instagram @zannakeithley.